HOW TO
AMERICAN

HOW TO AMERICAN

AN IMMIGRANT'S GUIDE
TO DISAPPOINTING YOUR PARENTS

JIMMY O. YANG
FOREWORD BY MIKE JUDGE

Da Capo Press

Da Capo Press
Hachette Book Group
1290 Avenue of the Americas, New York, NY 10104
www.dacapopress.com
@DaCapoPress

Printed in the United States of America

First Edition: April 2018
Published by Da Capo Press, an imprint of Perseus Books, LLC, a subsidiary of Hachette Book Group, Inc.

The Hachette Speakers Bureau provides a wide range of authors for speaking events. To find out more, go to www.hachettespeakersbureau.com or call (866) 376-6591.

The publisher is not responsible for websites (or their content) that are not owned by the publisher.

Editorial production by Christine Marra, *Marra*thon Production Services. www.marrathoneditorial.org

Book design by Jane Raese
Set in 12.5-point Dante MT

Cataloging-in-Publication Data is available from the Library of Congress
ISBN 978-0-306-90349-6 (hardcover)
ISBN 978-0-306-90350-2 (e-book)

LSC-C

10   9   8   7   6   5   4   3   2

CONTENTS

FOREWORD

When we first cast Jimmy O. Yang in *Silicon Valley*, I didn't know anything about him. I just had a good feeling about him based on his audition. I had no idea that the accent he was doing was not the way he normally spoke and that his persona was very different from that of the character he was playing in our show, Jian Yang. I also didn't know that he had graduated with a degree in economics from UCSD, the same school I graduated from many years earlier, or that he graduated in 2009, the year that I gave the commencement speech, and that he had attended it and apparently had been somewhat inspired to go into comedy by what I said. I found all this out after we had been working on set for a couple days.

Jimmy and I hit it off right away and became fast friends. As you'll notice when you read this book, he's a funny guy with an interesting and unique perspective on things in this country. You don't often hear the stories about Chinese immigrants. At least it seems that way to me. I think maybe it's because we Americans just don't ask. Jimmy and I hung out quite a bit and I became interested in his story. It's an interesting one. He's had quite a journey. From being a child Ping-Pong star in Hong Kong, to coming to America and becoming a stand-up comedian, achieving his dream of being a strip club DJ only to discover how sad and depressing that is, to becoming a successful TV and movie actor, Jimmy has really experienced America like few have.

When we were shooting the first season of *Silicon Valley*, we had no idea if the show would become a hit and go on for more seasons, or if it would flop and be quickly forgotten. We were all just working away trying our best to make it good and hoping it would work. Jimmy always had a great optimism about him, and when we'd talk about the show it would make my cynical ass believe that maybe it could be a hit.

And then it was. And as we went on to do additional seasons, Jimmy's character quickly became a cornerstone of the show. He also became my favorite character to write for around season three. There's something great and stoic about Jian Yang that Jimmy embodies perfectly. I know that sometimes language-barrier jokes can be considered easy by comedy snobs, but Jimmy makes it all work in a really great way.

I was already getting a sense that Jian Yang was becoming a favorite character on the show, but it really hit me when we were doing a panel at Comic-Con San Diego in 2016. We were in one of the big rooms with a couple thousand people (I'm bad with crowd numbers but it was at least that, maybe three or four thousand), and someone asked if there was going to be more Jian Yang next season. This was followed by thunderous applause, which was followed by even more thunderous applause when I said yes. Jimmy was officially famous.

Part of my inspiration for the show *Silicon Valley* came from back when I was working as an engineer. And at my first engineering job, I had an Iranian friend who worked there too, who said something that always stuck with me. He said that this really is the land of opportunity, but most Americans just don't see it because they're simply too used to it. They don't appreciate it and they don't take advantage of it as much as people who move here from other countries do. When you come to America from a place like Iran, you get here and you just marvel at all the opportunities and the freedom. Reading this book, you get the sense that Jimmy had that same experience, and he did not waste the opportunity at all. He worked his ass off for everything he has.

Jimmy's experience is uniquely American. You just don't hear these kinds of stories from other countries. Okay, somebody slap me. I'm getting too patriotic.

Here's something I'll never forget about Jimmy. Before the first season of *Silicon Valley* had aired, Jimmy and I were sitting at the bar at a restaurant in Santa Monica. (Now when I'm out with him, we are often interrupted by fans who recognize him and want to take selfies.) I was asking him about China. He was saying that if you're an ordinary American and you go to China, it's like being a movie star. Everyone stares at you and wants to be around you. He said it's the same if an American goes to Cuba. Then he paused for a second, looked down at his drink and said, "There's nowhere I can go." Well, Jimmy, now there's nowhere you *can't* go without being recognized like a star. Welcome to America, Jimmy O. Yang.

Mike Judge

PROLOGUE

"I eat the fish."

I said this to my roommate, in my thick Chinese accent.

"I know you eat the fish, but when you clean the fish, you can't just leave the fish head and guts and shit in the sink, because the whole house smells like a bait station. So you got to put it in the trash, then take the trash out. Do you understand?" my big, curly-haired American roommate explained to me, pointing at the leftover fish parts in the sink.

I stared at him, confused. And I replied, "Yes, I eat the fish."

"Motherfuck!" he howled in complete frustration.

The whole crew burst out in laughter. That was my second day on the set of *Silicon Valley,* an HBO show created by one of my comedy heroes, Mike Judge. It was my big break in Hollywood. My character, Jian Yang, is a fresh-off-the-boat Chinese immigrant whose struggle with the English language often leads to comical misunderstandings with his buffoonish roommate, Erlich Bachman, played by the impeccable T. J. Miller. It felt natural for me to play this character. I was once a fresh-off-the-boat Chinese immigrant myself. I was Jian Yang.

When my family immigrated to America from Hong Kong, I was a thirteen-year-old boy who looked like an eight-year-old girl. I didn't even speak enough English to understand the simplest American slang. On my first day of school in America, a girl came up to me and said:

"What's up?"

I stared at her, confused. I had never heard this term before.

She repeated, "What's up?"

I looked up into the sky to check "what is up" there. There wasn't anything. I looked back down at her and replied, "I don't know."

She finally realized I was either foreign or severely mentally handicapped. So she explained:

"'What's up?' means 'How are you doing?'"

"Oh, okay. I'm up. Thank you."

Then someone in the distance screamed out, "Heads up!" I turned to reply, thinking it was another American greeting. Instead, I was greeted by a weird oblong object flying right at me and hitting me straight in the gut; I later learned that was an American football.

This wasn't an episode of *Silicon Valley*; this was my life.

HOW TO
AMERICAN

CHAPTER ONE

HOW TO ASIAN

My life growing up in Hong Kong was like a bad stereotype. I played the violin, I was super good at math, and I played Ping-Pong competitively. In China, people take Ping-Pong seriously. It's not just a drunken frat house game; Ping-Pong is a prestigious national sport. The Ping-Pong champs in China are national heroes, like Brett Favre without the dick pics. Everyone from your five-year-old neighbor to your seventy-year-old aunt knows how to slice up some sick spins. My parents signed me up for Ping-Pong classes early on. I had quick feet and a lightning backhand. Soon I was competing in the thirteen-and-under Hong Kong championship leagues. I always had good form, but I was always smaller and weaker than the other kids. My dad would give me a pep talk before every match:

> "Jimmy, even though you are short, even though you are weak, and the other kid is way better than you . . . You are going to do okay."

He wasn't exactly Vince Lombardi, but thanks, Dad.

My tiny size eventually paid off when I was asked to test out a brand-new line of Ping-Pong tables with adjustable heights. They invited pro players to play with the kids and it was broadcast on the local news. It was a big deal. That was my big TV debut; I was ten years old. My perfect form and tiny stature made for an adorable display at the Ping-Pong table. The news camera found its way to me and gave me a personal close-up interview. The reporter asked me:

> "How do you like these new tables?"
> "I like them, because you can adjust them to be shorter, and I am short."

It was *soooooo* cute.

The next day, the news station called my family and asked me to come back for a full studio interview. This kid was a fucking star! I went on the show with my dad and crushed the interview. There were three cameras in the studio and I was a natural, swiveling my head from A camera to C camera, charming seven million people in Hong Kong with every line I uttered. Everyone thought I was the star Ping-Pong prodigy. I became the coolest kid in school and the pride and joy of my family. Everyone called me the golden-boy TV star. I felt like a celebrity. A few months later, I competed in a youth tournament representing my school. I was the favorite to win it all. But I faltered in front of the whole school. I lost 21–3 to a no-name newcomer, two matches in a row. Everybody was shocked; it was like Mike Tyson getting knocked out by Buster Douglas. The boy they once believed in was just a fraud. I couldn't back up my hype with my skills. I was definitely more a looker than a player. I was an imposter destined to be an actor.

I've always felt like an outsider, even as a Chinese kid growing up in Hong Kong. Hong Kong was a thriving British colony with its own government, and people in Hong Kong often looked down at their neighbors from Mainland China. Even though I was born in Hong Kong, my parents were mainlanders from Shanghai. I'd speak Cantonese in school, Shanghainese back home and watch TV shows in Mandarin. These Chinese dialects sounded as different as Spanish and Italian. My schoolmates in Hong Kong always called me "Shanghai boy." I had to stand up for myself when kids made fun of me for speaking to my parents in Shanghainese, wearing clothes from Shanghai and eating the Shanghainese food I brought to school. I didn't mind the teasing, but I'd always felt out of place, even in the city I was born in. This turned out to be some early practice on fitting in when we immigrated to America.

Everyone in Hong Kong has a legal Chinese name and an English nickname. My legal name is a four-character Chinese name. My family name is a rare two-character last name, 歐陽, *Ou Yang,* and my given name is 萬成, *Man Shing,* which means "ten thousand successes" in Chinese. It's a hopeful name that is sure to set me up for failure. No matter how successful I become, I can never live up to my parents' ten thousand ambitions. Jimmy was my English nickname given to me by my parents.

I grew up in a tight-knit nuclear family with my parents and an older brother. My mom's name was Amy, because it sounded close to her Chinese nickname *Ah-Mee.* My dad named himself Richard "because I want to be rich," he explained to me. And my brother was named Roger, after my parents fell in love with Roger Moore's portrayal of 007. Roger Ou Yang never liked his English name; he thought it sounded like an old white guy. So he changed his English name to Roy, an old black guy's name. I asked my parents why they named me Jimmy. They didn't really have an answer. My dad said, "It just sounded pretty good."

My mom is a fashionable lady who is too ambitious to be just a housewife. She was the stay-at-home mom turned career woman, becoming the general manager at a high-end clothing store in Hong Kong, aptly named Dapper. Mom is a people person but she is also very blunt. It's definitely a cultural thing. Asian ladies will tell you exactly what is wrong with your face, in front of your face, as if they were helping you. I always have to brace myself when I visit my parents. My mom often greets me with a slew of nonconstructive criticisms: "Jimmy ah, why is your face so fat? Your clothes look homeless and your long hair makes you look like a girl." After thirty years of this, my self-image is now a fat homeless lesbian.

Mom has always been a shrewd shopper. She's not cheap but it's all about finding a good deal. I once bought a fifty-dollar T-shirt at full price; she almost had a stroke.

"Jimmy! You spent fifty dollars on that shirt?! Are you crazy?! I can buy you five shirts in China for ten dollars!"

Then my dad tested the quality of the material by rubbing his thumb and index finger on the shirt. "Not even a hundred percent cotton. Garbage."

It took me a long time to come to terms with buying anything outside of Ross.

My dad is a sharp businessman and entrepreneur. He started a thriving medical equipment business in the early nineties in Hong Kong and then later became a financial adviser at Merrill Lynch when we came to America. He is the ultimate critic. He is a food critic, a movie critic and a people critic. Every restaurant we go to, he complains about the food, the service and even the utensils. He's like a walking Yelp review:

"The beef is tougher than a piece of cardboard. This is worse than the crap I ate during the Communist revolution."

"How are you going to call yourself a high-end restaurant if you use disposable chopsticks? I feel like I'm eating at Panda Express."

"The waiter is such an asshole. Why does he have red hair? He's fifty years old. He looks like a degenerate gambler."

The only restaurant he never complains about is Carl's Jr. He can devour two six-dollar burgers in one sitting, an impressive feat for anyone, especially a seventy-year-old Chinese dude.

Food is the glue in every Chinese family, and ours was no different. Chinese people are the biggest foodies in the world; there's a saying in China: "People put food first." We took dinner very seriously. There are always four homemade Chinese dishes and a gourmet soup du jour with a side of freshly made rice. Dad was serious about dinnertime. Every night at seven, he would yell at the top of his lungs, "Come eat dinner!" If we were a minute late, he would storm into me and my brother's FIFA game: "Do you want to eat or do you want to starve to death? Dinner. Now!" We wouldn't dare hit another button on the controller.

Dad was the head chef of the family. He specialized in Shanghainese cuisine, like his perfect recipe for red braised pork. Every day, Dad got off work at four and started cooking at five. My mother was a decent cook too, but every time she made dinner my dad would criticize her cooking. "Amy, this is too watery. You need to broil the mushrooms in high heat, not simmer in low heat." He relegated her cooking duties to an occasional simple tofu dish. Dad was actually a bit embarrassed by his cooking prowess. In the patriarchal Chinese culture, the woman is supposed to be the stay-at-home housewife and do all the cooking. Once in a while, Dad made sure to remind me, "Don't end up cooking in the kitchen like me, that should be a woman's job. But what am I supposed to do? I cook better than your mom." Some might call this misogyny; in my family it was irony.

My brother and I were responsible for cooking the rice. And there was nothing that made my dad angrier than fucking up the rice. The amount of water I put in the rice cooker could mean life or death. Cooking rice is an art form. If I put too little water in the cooker, the rice would be raw inside; if I put too much water in the cooker, the rice became a mushy porridge. It was a lot of pressure to make it right, because the entire five-course meal my dad whipped up depended on the consistency of the rice. Every night I felt like the pit crew member who had to change the tire of a Formula One race car. It was a thankless job, but if I fucked it up, I blew the entire race for everyone. I'd be nervously sitting at the dinner table, waiting for my dad to take the first bite of the rice. If it was cooked right, there would be no compliments, but if it was not cooked right:

"Motherfucker!" my dad would scream to the high heavens in Shanghainese. "This rice is raw. Who made the rice today?" And I'd shamefully raise my incapable hand. It was always my fault; my brother cooked the rice perfectly every time.

We never had space for a proper pet growing up in the small apartments in Hong Kong. When I was five, my brother and I got a couple of tadpoles, and we managed to raise them into frogs. That was our puppy. Then when I turned eight, my dad surprised us with a few fluffy warm-blooded pets: he came home with three pet chicks. They were the cutest little baby chickens. We put them in a spacious cage on our twentieth-floor balcony with a sweet view of the city. We weren't allowed to take them out and play with them because their pecks were rather painful. But we got to pet them through the cage and I used to stare at their cute fluffy yellow feathers for hours. We even gave them English names. My favorite was Gary; he was the smallest but the most energetic one. He reminded me of myself. Watching them grow was like watching a tadpole slowly transform into a frog. I was so proud of our progress. One day, I came home from school to visit little Gary and his friends, only to find the cage was empty. I panicked. I checked around the balcony, the living room, the bedrooms, and I couldn't find them anywhere. *Oh my God, did they fall off the balcony?* Then I went up to my dad in the kitchen:

"Dad, where is Gary?"
"He's right here."

Dad pointed to the wok in front of him, sizzling with fried chicken. And then I realized, Gary and his friends were never meant to be our pets; they were just farm-to-table dinner. I felt sick to my stomach. I was sure I would never be able to love again after that. I cried through dinner that night. But I have to admit: Gary was delicious.

Watching American action movies was the thing to do in Hong Kong. We were obsessed with all the larger-than-life American action heroes: Arnold, Stallone, Seagal and Van Damme. We watched *Terminator 2* every other weekend on our VCR. The opening sequence with the killer robot revolution scared the shit out of me, but then Arnold would drop out of the sky naked and save us all. One of our favorite local celebrities was Stephen

My dad RICH-ard, my brother Roger, aka Roy, my mom Ah-Mee and Jimmy the washed-up Ping Pong star.

Chow, a comedy legend in Hong Kong who later became an international star with *Shaolin Soccer* and *Kung Fu Hustle*. Stephen created a genre of comedy films in Hong Kong called *mo lei tau*. Translated from Cantonese, it literally means "nonsense." He mixed slapstick humor with his signature deadpan demeanor, much like Leslie Nielsen in the classic Jerry Zucker films like *Airplane* and *The Naked Gun*. Stephen was my hero and his *mo lei tau* films were my first comedy inspirations. My favorite film of his was *From Beijing with Love*, a spoof of the 007 series, featuring Stephen playing a bumbling low-end Chinese spy. The physical and prop humor were topnotch. The Chinese 007 pulls out a top-secret gadget kit. It has a mobile phone that is actually a shaver, a shaver that is actually a hairdryer and a hairdryer that is in fact a shaver. The creativity of these gags gave me some of my fondest childhood memories. Stephen Chow was my Hong Kong version of the Three Stooges, Laurel and Hardy and Peter Sellers.

HOW TO PURSUE YOUR DREAMS WITH ASIAN PARENTS

In America, people always tell me:

> "Money can't buy happiness. Do what you love."

In my Chinese family, my dad always tells me:

> "Pursuing your dreams is for losers.
> Doing what you love is how you become homeless."

The most important values in American culture are independence and freedom. The most important values in Chinese culture are family and obedience. And by no choice of my own, I am caught in between the two worlds. Having emigrated from Hong Kong to Los Angeles, I live my life in an often difficult duality. I grew up believing in the Chinese values my parents instilled in me, but I longed for the American value of pursuing what I loved. I have always been jealous of American kids and their freedom to do whatever they want. It's so simple for them; they don't have to follow a different set of Chinese rules back home. They get to frolic around the neighborhood streets and play in their tree houses by themselves with no parental supervision. My mom didn't even let me cross the street by myself. I had to hold her hand until I was fourteen years old. Asian parents are more protective than a lioness with her newborn cubs. Ever since we moved to America, I had to ask myself, *Am I Chinese or am I American?* I was caught between the two cultures and their polarizing beliefs. Should I follow my family's rules and be an obedient Chinese son, or should I follow my freedom and be an independent American man?

TOP FIVE CHINESE RULES

1. Respect your parents, your elders and your teachers. NEVER talk back or challenge them under any circumstance.

2. Education is the most important thing. It's more important than independence, the pursuit of happiness and sex.

3. Pay back your parents when you start working. We were all born with a student loan debt to our Asian parents. Asian parents' retirement plans are their kids.

4. Always call your elders "Uncle" or "Auntie," even if they are not related to you. NEVER call them by their first names.

5. Family first, money second, pursue your dreams never.

Whenever I tried to challenge my dad on his Chinese beliefs, he'd sternly put down the hammer: "You never ever talk to your father like that. It's disrespectful to challenge your father. I'd never dream of doing that to my father." How could I argue with that logic? So instead of forcing my parents to accept the American mindset, I quietly rebelled. I obeyed my parents' rules inside our Chinese household, while I pursued my dreams in the American world outside. I promised my parents I'd finish my college degree in economics, but then I turned down a job in finance to pursue a career in stand-up comedy after I graduated. My dad thought I was crazy. But I figured it was better to disappoint my parents for a few years than to disappoint myself for the rest of my life. I had to disappoint them in order to pursue what I loved. That was the only way to have my Chinese turnip cake and eat an American apple pie too.

When my parents found out I was frequenting comedy clubs, they prayed it was just a delusional phase I would grow out of. Bankers, doctors and scientists are what make Asian parents proud. Being an artist in China is the peasant work of a lowly clown. Stand-up isn't even a thing in China. My parents still refer to stand-up comedy as "talk show." My mom would ask me:

> "So you are doing your talk show tonight?"
> "Sure. Just like Jay Leno."
> I stopped correcting her after a while.

The closest form of stand-up in traditional Chinese culture is a two-man act called *xiang sheng,* or "crosstalk." It's a live stage act, usually made up of a big buffoonish character and a straight man doing sketch comedy routines, often singing along to a rhythm. It's like Laurel and Hardy meets Jay-Z, in Mandarin.

A few years ago, I finally mustered up the courage to invite my parents to my stand-up comedy show. It was at one of the nicest clubs I'd ever performed in: Brad Garrett's Comedy Club inside the MGM in Las Vegas. When I was ten, my family and I stayed at the MGM on a vacation from Hong Kong to Vegas, so surely my parents would know this was a legitimate five-star establishment. I sat them down at the best seat in the house and made sure all of their food and drinks were taken care of. They were the VIPs and I was the star that night. I had a killer set. Everyone in the audience was laughing head over heels. I finally proved to my parents that all the time I spent doing "talk shows" at comedy clubs wasn't in vain.

After the show, my parents came out and saw the crowd of adoring fans surrounding me. They waited in line with everyone, and I made sure to take my time greeting each audience member so they could see just how loved I was. When they finally reached the front of the line, my excited comedian friend Jack went up to my dad and asked him:

"So what do you think about your son? He was great, right?"

"No, he's not funny," my dad flatly replied. "I don't understand."

Jack's face dropped as he awkwardly looked over to me. But there were no tears on my face, not even a hint of surprise. Most people would have been devastated at their father's disapproval, but that was the exact answer I expected from my dad. I knew he wasn't going to understand stand-up. And I knew he was too honest to lie about how he felt. But I wasn't upset, because the joke was on him: I had spent the better half of my set making fun of him. This was exactly how I got my material. This exchange with my dad at the MGM would eventually make it into my set.

When my dad finally watched an episode of *Silicon Valley* he said, "I don't think your stand-up is funny, but I think *Silicon Valley* is very funny. You and your big white roommate are funny together." That's probably the nicest thing he'd ever say about my career. In a Chinese family, we never say, "I love you." That was his equivalent of a crying father hugging his son after winning the state championship football game. "I love you son, I'm so proud of you." After all, Dad wasn't a full-on hater. He didn't understand stand-up, but the dynamic between me and T. J. Miller on *Silicon Valley* was like the *xiang sheng* that he grew up with in China, and my deadpan delivery was like the Stephen Chow movies we watched back in Hong Kong.

My dad is also an actor. But I didn't come from an acting legacy like Angelina Jolie and Jon Voigt; Dad started acting after I did. When I finally started booking some roles he said, "If it's so easy you can do it, I can do it." *Fine, I'll show him how hard it is.* So I called my agent, Jane, the next day and asked if she'd be interested in signing my dad. "Sure, I can use an old Asian guy on my roster," Jane said. Apparently old Asian dudes are rare commodities in Hollywood. This would surely show him the trials and tribulations I had to go through to become an actor. I'd give it a month before he called it quits on these grueling auditions. Two weeks later, the old man started booking everything. He booked four out of his first six auditions, an unheard of success rate. My dad called me, "I booked another one! This is so easy, why isn't everybody doing it!" My dad was a natural and I was a struggling actor. My plan completely backfired.

One of the roles he booked was playing a Chinese mob boss on a Chinese television show called *Little Daddy*. It was a meaty three-episode arc that shot in San Francisco. I didn't think much of it when he landed the role, assuming it was probably some second-tier production. *Little Daddy* became one of the most popular shows in China. It went on to sweep the hearts of a billion Chinese people. All of our relatives and family friends from China called and congratulated my dad on his brilliant performance. My aunt from Shanghai called him and exclaimed, "Richard! You were so good in that role! Your son must have taken after you! I hope he succeeds just like you." I fucked up.

However, this apparent curse did eventually lead to an unlikely breakthrough for me. When my dad was killing it as the hottest old Asian dude to hit Hollywood since Mr. Miyagi, I was scraping together small, two-line parts on TV. Then my dad got an audition to be a scientist on one of my favorite TV shows, *It's Always Sunny in Philadelphia*. It was a prominent role and they were looking for an older actor to play a Mandarin-speaking scientist. I was so jealous of this opportunity, and my dad had never even heard of the show. When he called me the night before to run lines with him, I reluctantly agreed. It felt like a girl that you like calling you to tell you about another guy she likes; it was pretty painful. The next morning, Jane, our agent, gave me a call. She asked bluntly, "Hey, do you think your dad can handle this role? It's a lot of dialogue in Mandarin and English."

"Yeah, I think he'll be fine." That was half a lie. My dad might have been killing it in his earlier auditions, but they were mostly commercials and Chinese television. This was a comedic part on an American improvised comedy show. But I vouched for my old man because, well, he's my old man.

But Jane's agent spidey sense was tingling. "Maybe I'll call the casting director and tell them to bring you in and read for the part instead."

I couldn't say no, but I also didn't want to throw my dad under the bus, so I just passively responded, "Whatever works."

"Okay, I'll call them." Now I had less than two hours to prepare for the audition for myself, and I also had to explain to my dad what happened. I called him right away to catch him before Jane.

> "Hey, Dad, I think Jane wants me to audition for the
> part instead," I said sheepishly, waiting for him to punch
> me through the phone.
> "I think that's good, I don't think I'm ready anyway.
> You will do better than me."

I was surprised by this rare moment of vulnerability from my dad. This time, he ran the lines with me. I didn't have time to second-guess myself when I went into the casting office. *What do I have to lose?* This wasn't my part to begin with. Then I got the part, my biggest role yet, on one of my favorite comedy shows, thanks to my dad. And it just so happened that particular episode, "Flowers for Charlie," was written by the writers/executive producers of my favorite drama on TV, *Game of Thrones*, David Benioff and D. B. Weiss. I fanboyed super hard when we took a group photo with my favorite drama show creators and my favorite comedy show actors. David, DB, the gang from *Always*

Sunny and I posed inside of the gang's pub. My dad becoming an actor led to one of the brightest highlights of my acting career.

LEFT TO RIGHT: Glenn Howerton, D. B. Weiss, David Benioff, Asian kid who took the job from his dad, Charlie Day and Rob McElhenney.

Three years later, I made my big-screen debut in *Patriots Day*. I returned the favor and got my dad a role to play my dad in the movie. In the drama I played the based-on-real-life hero Danny Meng, the Chinese immigrant who was carjacked by the two terrorist brothers responsible for the Boston Marathon bombing. It was an honor to play Danny and get to know him in real life. Peter Berg was the director and Mark Wahlberg was a producer and the star of the film. We made sure to portray every detail accurately to honor the real-life victims and heroes of the tragedy. When Danny is first introduced in the film, he is facetiming his parents back home in Sichuan, China, speaking Mandarin.

Originally, they cast a Chinese actor from Boston to play my dad, but unbeknownst to the filmmakers, he spoke Mandarin with a thick Cantonese accent. Since I was born in Hong Kong to parents from Mainland China, I was fluent in both dialects. Although the American audience wouldn't know the difference between Cantonese and Mandarin, it meant a lot to me to get it right for the Chinese-speaking viewers. Pete trusted me and agreed to recast the dad. And I asked him, "What about my dad? He's an actor." They flew my dad out to Boston the following week. He played the scene brilliantly. It was a big deal for my dad to make his feature debut and share this experience with his son.

On the set of *Patriots Day* with director Peter Berg, my fake mom and my real dad.

One of the shining moments of my life was taking my parents to the *Patriots Day* premiere at the world-famous Grauman's Chinese Theatre on Hollywood Boulevard. We shared the red carpet with all the stars from the film, Mark Wahlberg, Kevin Bacon, J. K. Simmons, John Goodman and Michelle Monaghan. I couldn't believe I was part of this incredible cast, and so was my dad. It was wonderful to share the red carpet with my parents and sit by them when they watched my movie debut. The highlight of the night was the after-party. My parents and I were seated across from Kevin Bacon, who is officially one degree separated from me. (Sorry, I know this joke is played out, but I had to.) My dad kept nudging me in the arm and whispered, "Hey, you think we can take a picture with Kevin Bacon?" *For once in my life, I'm on the same level with Kevin Bacon, why can't I just enjoy it? I don't want to be a fanboy!* But I relented, knowing that selfie would mean a lot to my parents. So I went up to Kevin with my parents satellited around me. "Hey, Kevin, nice to meet you." This was the first time we'd met, since we didn't have any scenes together in the film.

"Hey!" Mr. Bacon enthusiastically replied. "Nice to meet you too."

"Kevin, these are my parents, and they are big fans of yours. Can we take a picture with you?"

"Of course!"

Kevin was incredibly nice. He leaned in and said to my dad:

"So, what do you think about your son in the movie— he was great, right?"

Oh no! Kevin Bacon is making the same mistake Jack made outside of the comedy club in the MGM.

I braced myself for my dad's response:

"Yes, yes, my son was in the movie. You know, I was in the movie too."

Dad was too busy giving himself a plug, instead of throwing me under the bus. Thank God. He took out his phone and snapped a selfie.

All the years of disappointments from my parents seemed to have vanished after this Kevin Bacon selfie. To see them happy was a bigger achievement than any accolade I could get from Kevin Bacon. I've learned to embrace my dad as a fellow actor, but he'll never see me as an actor; I'll always be his son who fucked up the rice.

This fanboy moment has turned out to be one of our favorite family portraits.

CHAPTER TWO

HOW TO
IMMIGRANT

My family emigrated from Hong Kong to Los Angeles in 2000, when I was thirteen years old. Thirteen is an awkward transitional period for any prepubescent teen. Not only did I have to learn about my newly found pubes, I had to move to a new country, learn a new language and assimilate into a new culture.

My parents moved to America hoping for a better college education for my brother and me. To most foreigners, America has the most prestigious universities and the best job opportunities for college graduates. Ironically, the only people who might disagree with that sentiment are people who actually live in America. The grass is always greener and the college diplomas are always shinier from a different country. Even though Hong Kong is one of the biggest metropolitan cities in the world, it just doesn't seem to have the same opportunities America has. You can make it big as a banker, a real estate developer and a doctor in Hong Kong, but you can literally be an astronaut, a rock star or anything you want in America. We moved here believing in the American dream.

Los Angeles seemed like an easy choice for my family. My aunt and my grandparents had already immigrated and they had lived in LA for more than ten years. And my parents wanted my brother and me to go to USC or UCLA, both of which later rejected me. At least my brother is now a proud UCLA graduate, so the immigration wasn't a total loss for my parents.

I was scared to leave the only place I'd known, but I couldn't wait to see all the massive mansions, fancy sports cars and beautiful people that I'd seen in Hollywood movies. I thought I was going to be neighbors with Harrison Ford, Brad Pitt and Jennifer Aniston. The first day my family got to Los Angeles, we visited my grandparents in Beverly Hills. But it wasn't anything fancy like I had expected from Beverly Hills. They lived in a quaint little four-unit apartment complex on the edge of town. We walked up some old misshapen stairs to their unit. Coming from the skyscrapers in Hong Kong, I was very amused by this little two-story building. I'd never been to anyone's home that didn't require taking an elevator. The apartment had a dull dusty scent; it was some kind of old-people stench. I used to call it "Grandpa smell." It was a small space and my grandparents had put a familiar Chinese touch to it. From the kitchen to the living room, it was filled with Chinese newspapers, Chinese food and furniture from China you'd never see in other American households, like this small plastic stool you'd squat on in the kitchen; people used it to prep the food on the floor level. You can only find that in China. It was a classic Chinese immigrant's home where Chinese décor met American architecture.

That day, Grandpa took my dad and me to his favorite restaurant in Los Angeles. I was ready for my very first American feast and I was excited to explore Tinsel Town. Three generations of Chinese strolling down the beautiful streets of LA. We walked down La Cienega Boulevard, a main artery of LA. Every building we passed by was wide and short. In Hong Kong, every building was slim and at least twenty stories tall. That's the only way to cram seven million people on an island the size of San Diego. It was nice to leave the concrete jungle and see the wide-open California sky, but at the same time Los Angeles felt a bit empty and lacking in humanity. There were only a few pedestrians on the streets; it was eerily vacant compared to the human sardine can I was used to in Hong Kong. The streets were massive gray pavements with six lanes of traffic and a narrow sidewalk. This was definitely a town built for cars, not humans. We walked by a few strip malls with dreary dry cleaners and generic burger shops. I'd never seen a strip mall before. Every mall in Hong Kong was a monstrous shopping center that stretched vertically for multiple levels. These monotonous strip malls with flat white paint looked like the lonesome Wild West with the proverbial tumbleweed rolling by.

Finally, we walked by a Pizza Hut, one of my favorite restaurants back in Hong Kong. I asked Grandpa:

"Can we eat here?"

"You can't eat here, there's nowhere to sit."

I didn't realize this Pizza Hut was just a kitchen for pizza delivery. *What a fraud!* The Pizza Hut in Hong Kong was a nice sit-down restaurant with a swanky salad bar. You could order pizzas with shrimp, a fancy pie-crust soup and my favorite seafood pasta. This American version of a pizza oven inside of a hole in the wall was quite jarring to me. *How is the authentic version so much shittier than the foreign version?* I felt betrayed.

Fifteen minutes into our supposedly ten-minute walk, I asked my grandpa in Shanghainese, "Are we there yet?" It's a universal saying amongst impatient children around the world, in all languages.

"We are very close, just a few more minutes." We ended up walking for forty-five minutes in the sweltering dry heat of a Los Angeles summer.

We finally arrived at our destination. It was the biggest strip mall yet. On one side, there was a huge two-story building called LA Fitness. I wasn't quite familiar with the concept of gyms yet. We didn't have corporate gyms in Hong Kong; everyone was skinny. On the other side of the strip mall, there was a small glass building. Grandpa pointed to it and said, "This is it, my favorite restaurant in LA. It's authentic Mexican cuisine; they don't have this in China." I looked up at the sign:

EL POLLO LOCO

I had never heard of El Pollo Loco. I didn't even know the name was in Spanish; I thought it was three English words I hadn't learned yet. I was disappointed that a forty-five-minute hike ultimately ended in a fast food joint. But once we walked in, I realized this place was unlike any fast food restaurant I'd ever been to. I saw the biggest grill I'd ever seen in my life behind the registers, packed with rows of whole chickens with a beautiful brownish yellow tint. It smelled absolutely delicious. I looked through the glass panel and I saw a cornucopia of sides: rice, beans, mac and cheese, corn and an interesting green substance, which I later learned was called guacamole.

My grandpa went up to order in his Shanghai English:"Six pieces, dark meat."

Then he turned around and explained to us in Shanghainese:

"They let you choose which part of the chicken you want here, dark meat and white meat. Dark meat is the good parts. White meat is the breast. It's dry and rough for American idiots."

Grandpa's words of wisdom. To this day, I still only order dark meat.

Then the cashier asked Grandpa:

"Flour or corn?"

"Flour."

And once again, he turned around and explained it to us in Shanghainese: "They give you these bread sheets to wrap your chicken in. Flour is good. The corn ones taste funny." After a college trip to Tijuana, I realized the corn ones didn't taste funny, they tasted authentic. I now strictly order corn tortillas. Sorry, Grandpa.

Grandpa finished the order with three cups of water. He said to us, "They make their money by overcharging you on soda. You can just get a free water cup and fill it with whatever you want." My mind was fucking blown. *You can pour your own soda here? And it's free? Wow!* Jesus could turn water into wine, but in America you could turn water into Dr Pepper. What a beautiful country.

Then there was the salsa bar. What can I say about the salsa bar that hasn't been said about Disneyland? It was a magical kingdom of color and flavor. The El Pollo Loco salsa bar exemplified American freedom; land of the free, home of the salsa bar. "Take whatever you want, it's free," Grandpa said. I thought he was messing with me. I looked at that salsa bar in front of me like a virgin staring at a naked Gigi Hadid.

This can't be. This is too good to be true.

Grandpa noticed my hesitation and he nudged me forward. "Go ahead. Take as much as you want. Take some home if you want to." *Why would anyone ever buy onions and cilantro if it's already finely chopped and free for the taking here in El Pollo Loco?!* If I had known what the word *loco* meant, I would have understood. There is so much freedom in this fast food joint, it's *loco*! El Pollo Loco was the most American place I'd ever been to.

After stuffing ourselves full of dark meat and free salsa, we had to walk the same forty-five minutes back to my grandpa's apartment. This was way before Uber. I was exhausted that night, but I couldn't sleep. My first day of American school was tomorrow and the only thing I knew about America was *El Pollo Loco.*

The first day I walked into John Burroughs Middle School, I felt like Andy Dufresne getting off the bus and walking into Shawshank prison. John Burroughs was a middle school in the LA Unified School District that went from sixth to eighth grade. I was thirteen years old, which placed me in the eighth and last grade of the school. Which meant I started in this school where everyone had already known each other for at least two years. It's always scary for a new kid to move to a new school; I was a new foreign kid moving to a new school on a new continent. I was scared, confused and anxious. A part of me wanted to keep to myself, but another part of me desperately wanted to make some new friends. I was never shy with strangers, but this was an entirely different world. It was a different culture, a different language and a different educational system. It was like I was transported to an alternate universe.

Before classes started, I walked through the exercise yard where all the kids hung out. This would be what they called gen-pop, or general population in prison. In Hong Kong, we only had Chinese kids in school. In John Burroughs, there were kids of every race, every religion and every size. I had never interacted with white people, black people or Hispanic people before. I didn't even know where to start. Then, I was relieved to see a group of Asian kids who looked like my friends back home. I walked up to them to introduce myself in my native tongue, but when I got close enough I realized they were speaking Korean. I froze and walked away with my tail between my legs. My hopes were crushed. I soon realized that all the Asian kids in this school were Koreans. I wasn't racist; I just didn't know how to speak enough English to have a conversation yet. I had learned English in Hong Kong the way American high school kids learn Spanish. I knew some vocabulary words, but I couldn't carry on a conversation; it felt like everyone was speaking way too fast. I was desperately hoping for some Chinese kids I could cling on to in this new school. In hindsight, this was a blessing in disguise. If I had gone to an American school with a lot of other Chinese kids, I would not have been forced to assimilate, and I would have probably turned out to be the dude selling dim sum in Chinatown.

I made my way to the basketball courts. I was a pretty good basketball player back home, so I was hoping to show off some of my skills and earn some first-day respect. For a fleeting moment, Yao Ming blocked Shaquille O'Neal and I thought I could be a baller in the NBA. But for the sobering fact that I was two feet too short, I really thought I could have made it. Then I saw Marquees. Marquees was an eighth grader who was six two and looked like he was twenty-five; he was a grown-ass man. As I walked towards the hoop, he ran by me in a blur and took off into the air for a monster slam-dunk. My jaw dropped to the hot cement. I'd only seen NBA players do that on TV. *You are telling me regular thirteen-year-old kids can do this in America?* My mind could not comprehend this superhuman athleticism. I scurried off of the court without making eye contact with anyone. My hoop dreams were crushed. Marquees's dunk made me feel inadequate as a man.

Before first period, I landed in something called the "home room," a weirdly useless class that briefed its students before they went off to their real classes. Before I even had a chance to settle into my seat, we were all asked to rise up from our chairs. I'm not sure if I understood any of the instructions; I just followed what the other kids were doing. Everyone put their right hand on their chest and looked up to an American flag in the front of the classroom. Then everyone started to chant, "I pledge allegiance to the flag of the United States of America . . ." I was lost. I looked around at my peers and I saw everyone all uniformly saying the same thing. I thought to myself, *Did I just join a cult or something?* I had no idea what those words meant. I just pretended to move my lips so I didn't seem out of place. It was a nerve-wracking two minutes for me. I hadn't met any of my classmates yet, and I didn't want someone to notice the foreign kid wasn't doing something that everyone else was doing. All I wanted to do was fit in, but the Pledge of Allegiance made me feel more foreign than ever. Finally, everyone sat down, and I breathed a sigh of relief. Unknowingly, that was the moment I became an American.

Next, the teacher did a roll call. *Oh good*, I thought, *this is something I can handle. We did roll calls in Hong Kong too. How different can this be?* The older white lady teacher started to call out the names: "Marcus Johnson." "Here!" "Suzy Kim." "Here!" "Man Sh—Shing, Ouuuy—ann—?" The rest of the class looked around for this unfamiliar newcomer. I raised my hand before she could butcher my name any further. "Here. You can call me Jimmy." I nervously looked around the room and I saw everyone whispering to each other, discussing this new little Chinese boy. The teacher said, "Welcome, Jimmy." I certainly didn't feel very welcome.

Physical education class was the first period after home room. PE had always been my favorite class in Hong Kong. Even though I looked like a tiny nerd, I'd always gravitated towards sports. I might never be able to dunk like Marquees but I was confident that I could drain some three-pointers and score me some new friends. After all, how different could PE class be in America? Before hitting the field in PE class, we had to go to the locker room to change into our gym clothes. I'd never changed in front of other people before, so I waited until everyone else took off their pants before I did. I made myself as invisible as possible and tried to change faster than a new fish taking a prison shower. Then a kid next to me laughed out loud and said, "Are you wearing tighty whities? Dude, that's fucking gay."

Everyone looked over and started laughing at me. I couldn't have been more embarrassed by my tighty whities fresh out of Hong Kong. I hopped into my gym shorts as quickly as possible. Then, the same kid screamed out, "Pull down your shorts!" I was so confused. *I just put them on.* I stared at him blankly and said, "What?"

He blurted out again, much more insistent this time, "Pull down your shorts, man!" I looked around and everyone was seemingly agreeing with his comment. I went into full panic mode. *Am I about to get booty raped like they show in the American prison movies? Is this how they initiate new kids in Los Angeles public schools?*

I didn't know what to do, so I slowly pulled down my gym shorts. As they got past my knees, the kid said, "Yo, what the fuck are you doing? Don't pull it down all the way, just sag it." I looked at him, befuddled, with my shorts halfway down my legs. Then he pointed to his own shorts. "Sag your pants a little so you don't look like a nerd. Nobody pulls their pants all the way up." I had no idea what he was talking about. I just blindly followed his instructions to pull my shorts halfway down my butt to showcase a little bit of my tighty whities.

I later learned that sagging was an American trend from the hip-hop community. Rappers would wear loose pants hanging halfway down their ass, so they could look like a cool gangster who just got out of prison. Every kid in America was doing it. Pulling your shorts all the way up was called the John Stockton, a super white NBA basketball player from the Utah Jazz in the nineties. Lame. So I waddled around the rest of the class with my waistband around my anus. I thought I looked like I had just crapped my pants, but apparently that was super cool. What did I know? I was a foreign kid who was trying to fit in any way I could. I was just relieved that wasn't the day I lost my virginity.

Now that my shorts were halfway sagged and my dignity was still somewhat intact, I was ready for some sporting. Much to my dismay, we had to play American football that day. I'd never touched a football in my life, and I didn't even know what the Super Bowl was. I had tried to watch an American football game once. It had so many rules that it was impossible to understand. *What is a first down? What the hell is a pass interference?* It sounded like a made-up sport some bros came up with when they were wasted. Like one guy said, "Bro, you can't push me when I'm catching the ball. That's like, pass interference, bro." That's how most foreigners see American football.

I was lost on the field. Marquees was throwing the ball, or as I later learned, playing the so-called quarterback. I stood wide open in the middle of the field because nobody bothered to cover the little foreign kid in tighty whities, but Marquees took a chance on my tiny geisha hands. He flung the ball in a hard spiral right at my chest with his cannon of an arm. With the quick reaction time I had developed from Ping-Pong, I miraculously caught the ball by pinning it against my body. It was thrown so hard, the momentum took me to the ground. I lay flat on my back clutching the football, not sure what had just happened. Then Marquees stood over me and said, "Good catch! First down!" And that was when I fell in love with American football. Now I am in three fantasy football leagues and I watch seven hours of the NFL every Sunday with a six-pack of Bud Light like a red-blooded American, screaming, "First down!"

There were these two scoundrels in my PE class, David and Diego. Some might call them bullies; I just thought these dudes were douchebags who talked a lot of shit. Nothing I couldn't handle. Every day in PE class, David and Diego would fire off some trash talk to me, usually along the lines of my mama being fat. I was never bothered by the words, knowing that my mother was a skinny woman.

One day, we were all waiting in line to hit some baseballs. David and Diego just wouldn't stop. They kept making stupid comments to me and then laughing amongst themselves at my expense. Then, Diego got really close to me and started whispering the trash talk into my ear. "Your mom is a fatass," he whispered. The words didn't bother me but his hot breath in my ear got on my nerves and it triggered something primal inside of me. I did something I'd never done in my life. I kicked his ass. I'd never taken any martial arts classes, but there must have been something embedded in my Chinese DNA. Out of instinct, I turned around and round-house kicked Diego square in the gut. He gasped and folded over. Then I jumped up as high as I could, and I came down with a massive karate chop to the back of the neck. He collapsed onto his knees. My adrenaline was pumping and I was ready to finish him. David quickly jumped in between us and screamed, "Stop! Stop!" I stood still in my kung fu stance and stared them down. I saw the fear in their eyes as David picked Diego up from the ground. David said to him:

"Don't fuck with this kid, he's fucking Bruce Lee."
From that day on, nobody said one more word about my mama ever again.

THE PUBLIC SCHOOL HUSTLE

In second-period science class, I sat across from Juan Menjivar. He was like the Mexican Bart Simpson, a notorious troublemaker. He wasn't the nicest kid per se, but he was fun to be around. He would always make fun of people and disrupt the class. The teachers thought he was a nightmare, but I've always seen him as a friend; in fact, one of my first friends in America. I became friends with Juan when we struck a business deal early in the school year when he sold me his lunch tickets. Juan had government-issued lunch tickets; they are basically food stamps for students from underprivileged households. Each ticket could be exchanged for a free lunch that normally cost five dollars and Juan would sell his tickets for three dollars. He would go up and down the lunch line every day and ask, "Does anyone need a ticket?" I always thought you'd be a fool not to buy from these lunchtime pushers. You got the same exact lunch for a two-dollar discount. Even my mom would think that was a good deal. So I quickly raised my hand and said, "Yeah, I'll take one." Juan became my lunch ticket dealer for every lunch in John Burroughs.

A few weeks went by and I thought I should strike a long-term deal with Juan to lock in my savings. So I proposed to Juan, "I'll buy your whole week's tickets, and I'll pay you ten bucks for them on Monday. This way, you don't have to come out here and work every day. You can just have ten bucks every week and enjoy your lunchtime." Juan tried to make some calculations in his head but he soon gave up; the American public school system has failed him. He said, "Okay, ten bucks, but you have to give me your chocolate milk every day." Without hesitation I said, "Deal." I didn't care much for my Alta Dena boxed milk anyway and I could use the extra dollar I saved to buy whatever soda I wanted. That was the first open-trade agreement between China and Mexico on American soil.

I was owning these publicly educated kids in the lunchroom and I was owning the public school curriculum in the classroom. Soon I became an honors student at John Burroughs. I didn't think I was particularly special; the American education system was just particularly easy compared to the high-pressure educational system in Hong Kong. In the States, most kids are still learning the multiplication table in seventh grade. In Hong Kong, we've all learned algebra by sixth grade. Aside from English, every subject in the US was at least two years behind compared to Hong Kong. My family came to this country hoping for the best college education, but we didn't realize how pedestrian the public school system was leading up to it. I didn't mind that at all. I figured I could just cruise through school and score some easy As. I was like a twenty-year-old Dominican baseball player using a fake birth certificate to play in Little League. But my parents had other plans. They wanted me to be on the fast track; they wanted me to be in the so-called Magnet Program. So my dad went to have a chat with the principal. Dad took me to school and he brought all my textbooks. He stormed into the principal's office and slammed the textbooks on the principal's desk.

"My son has learned this already. He is smart. You need to put him in the smartest classes."

The principal was intimidated by this middle-aged Asian man with a comb-over. She responded:

"Your son is on a good track, he is already in the
advanced math class."
"That's too easy, when can he learn calculus? What
about game theory?"

My dad had this weird obsession with game theory, an advanced mathematical prediction model. To him, that was like the Holy Grail of high-end math. I did end up learning it in college, but I've forgotten all about it because like most things they taught me in school, it was completely useless. The principal said, "the highest-level math class we have is algebra, the best I can do is put him in the algebra class."

Dad turned to me and asked, "Do you already know algebra?"

I hesitated for a second. Then I replied, "No, not really."

I lied. I had already learned algebra in Hong Kong, but I wanted to continue my scam through the American school system. I soon became an honor student, and my dad proudly rocked a MY SON IS AN HONOR STUDENT IN JOHN BURROUGHS MIDDLE SCHOOL bumper sticker on the back of his Pontiac Grand Am. I would say that's a win-win.

John Burroughs Middle School
STUDENT OF THE MONTH
Ou Yang Man Shing

NOVEMBER 2000

Presented for Exceptional improvement in class

Principal *Fonna Bishop*

Scammer of the month.

Good grades were nice, but I wanted much more than that. I wanted to be accepted by my peers; I wanted girls; I wanted to experience the American teenage life.

I had gone to an all-boys school from first to seventh grades in Hong Kong, so I'd had literally zero interactions with the opposite sex. Now I was thrown into a brand new country, with a different language, white girls who were six inches taller than me. Multiply all that by the awkwardness of puberty, forget about it. I had no chance. I was more lost than a dog watching *Game of Thrones*. There was this really cute girl at John Burroughs named Ally, or so I was told. She was a tall skinny white girl who looked like Molly Sims, every Asian man's dream. She was the all-American beauty. I stared at her every day during lunch, wishing I had enough courage to just say hi to her. She would sit by the basketball courts with her friends and I would stand twenty yards away at the lunch tables, secretly admiring her. It kind of sounds creepy now, but I was in eighth grade; it was super cute.

Juan would egg me on. "Just go talk to her, man! It's not a big deal." It was the biggest deal in my mind; it was life and death. "Just go!" He pushed me in the back and I stumbled two steps forward. I was so scared that I quickly cowered back to my safe distance. I firmly stood my feeble ground. Juan continued, "Okay fine, I'll go talk to her, and tell her 'Jimmy really likes you.'" I grabbed his arm so hard he could have dislocated his shoulder. "No!" I shouted. That was perhaps my only chance, and I was too scared to even have a friend talk to her for me. And for the rest of the school year, I stared at her from a distance as if I had a restraining order. And for the rest of my teenage years, I dreamt about having a girl like Ally.

I kept my easy-grade scam going and graduated John Burroughs with straight As, and I got my lunch on a government discount through Juan. I survived my first year in America by constantly assimilating and adapting. It was exhausting. But my family was the one constant that kept me sane. Whenever I felt lost in school, I could always count on coming home for a home-cooked Shanghainese dinner. It was a blessing to have a buffer year at middle school before being judged by the unforgiving teenage peers in high school. It was a year of American cultural boot camp, a year for me to learn English, a year for me to assimilate. I went into high school with my pants sagged, reciting the Pledge of Allegiance and ready to catch some footballs. 'Murica!

CHAPTER THREE

HOW TO
THUGLIFE

My nuclear family has always been the rock in my ever-changing life. We settled into our new lives after our first year in America. My dad had gotten a steady job as a financial adviser, my mom worked as a teller for a Chinese bank and my brother got into UCLA. On the surface, everything was seemingly working out perfectly for this immigrant family. But while I was trying to fit in in school, my parents were dealing with their own struggles as adult immigrants. My dad landed a job as a financial adviser at Merrill Lynch, but it was a commission-based job. He didn't know many people here in America yet, let alone people who would trust him to invest their money. He always acted like everything was fine, but I could hear the arguments between him and my mom about the mounting credit card debts. I felt responsible being a vestige in that household, and I stopped asking for the newest Jordans or the newest video games. I'd rather wear flip-flops to school than be homeless.

Mom had an especially hard time assimilating to America. Her English wasn't very sharp and the language barrier kept her from getting the jobs she wanted. She took a job as a menial bank teller in a Chinese bank twenty miles away, barely making minimum wage. Aside from hanging with some family friends, she never found her footing in the community. Mom was often quite lost during English conversations; she'd just politely nod and smile. When a foreign person doesn't understand something, instead of saying, "Pardon me" they'll just nod their head and smile "yeah, yeah, yeah." Behind that cordial smile, I knew she felt terribly uncomfortable.

Mom got a job offer from Shanghai two years after we moved to LA. It was a general manager position at a chic clothing store opened by a famous Chinese artist. It was exactly the kind of job she loved and thrived at back in Hong Kong. It'd be a sizable pay raise from being a bank teller, and some much needed income for the family. But this would also mean she'd have to move to Shanghai, without us. We had a serious family discussion on whether or not she should take the job and go to Shanghai. I still remember that day vividly. Dad is an old-school guy. He wanted her to stay because there was nothing more important than keeping the family together, but I knew her mind was already made up. She said to me:

> "Jimmy, ah, I'm just going there for work. I will always come back and visit." The thought of her being a visitor in my life was devastating. I cried.
>
> "Mom, I don't want you to go. But do whatever you want."
>
> I stormed into my room and buried my face in my pillow. She left for Shanghai a week later, and she lived there for the next ten years.

I was sad, angry and confused. Deep down I understood why she left, but it was way too much for a fifteen-year-old to process. Mom's decision to go to Shanghai was the first time the four of us had ever been separated. Being the youngest in the family, it hit me especially hard. I was raised to be the obedient Chinese boy, but my mom seemed to have chosen the American independent spirit to pursue her dreams. I didn't know what to believe anymore. It took me a long time to come to terms with her leaving. I felt hurt, I felt resentful and I felt abandoned by my own mother. The first night after she left, my brother was out with his college friends, so it was just my dad and me at the dinner table. It felt awfully empty. The usually joyous and rowdy family dinner table was completely silent. My dad tried his best to help me cope with this, in his matter-of-fact way. "It's just me and you now. Mom is not coming back. Get used to that. Eat." I couldn't swallow a bite that night.

Mom would call us to check in every night when it was daytime in Shanghai, but I didn't want to talk to her. My dad literally had to press the phone to my face so I'd say hi and bye. She came back for a month every year but I couldn't really enjoy that time, knowing she was just going to leave again. The world didn't look quite the same anymore. The contentment I found at home was gone. My family, the only thing I could count on to be a constant in my life, had changed just like everything else. I couldn't be the obedient Chinese family boy anymore, even if I wanted to; I had no choice but to grow up and be an independent American man.

90210

After graduating from John Burroughs Middle School, I was on track to go to Fairfax High School in the Los Angeles Unified School District. My dad might be foreign, but he knew the LAUSD was a cesspool full of gangs, metal detectors and teenage pregnancy. So in an act of brilliance and desperation, he used my grandpa's address to register my school district, so I could go to the prestigious Beverly Hills High School, the alma mater of Hollywood stars like Angelina Jolie, Betty White and John Travolta.

I didn't care about all the posh stigma of Beverly Hills; I was just glad that I got a second chance to establish who I was in a brand new school district. In John Burroughs, I'd solidified myself as the foreign kid who didn't know how to sag his pants. Now I had a chance to use the American training I'd learned in middle school to show everyone I knew all the words to the Pledge of Allegiance like it was a Britney Spears song.

Beverly Hills High was nothing like the TV show 90210. First of all, not everyone was white and they didn't look like they were thirty-five. Most people picture Beverly Hills High as this glamorous high school with beautiful teenagers who have very cool adult problems; in reality, it was just a public school with a ton of Persian kids who drove Beamers. It was also a predominately Jewish school, which was awesome because we had all the Jewish holidays off as well as the Christian holidays. While other kids were praying and fasting during their days off on Rosh Hashanah and Passover, I was happily playing *Grand Theft Auto* and eating pork chops.

In high school, everyone was part of a clique, and they had a specific hangout spot at lunch. The cool athletes sat in front of the swim gym, the skaters sat on the front lawn and the Persians with Phat Beamers roamed the cafeteria. It was like the scene in *Clueless* where Alicia Silverstone introduces all the groups. As a matter of fact, research for *Clueless* was done at Beverly Hills High School, and our real English teacher Mr. Hall played the principal who introduces Brittany Murphy in the movie. That was his claim to fame in Hollywood and everybody in school thought Mr. Hall was a big-time celebrity. As the new fish that didn't come from the Beverly Hills elementary school track, I was once again among a sea of strangers. I didn't know anyone going into my first day of high school and I didn't belong to any of those cliques. With no place to hang out at lunch, I just stood with my back against the lockers, hoping nobody would notice me, quietly eating my weird Chinese lunch that my dad had packed for me. My usual lunch was Chinese food my dad made from the night before packed into a Tupperware; anything from pork belly with pickled vegetables to eel braised in soy sauce. Once a week, my dad packed me a hot pocket. It wasn't your normal American Hot Pocket with ham and cheese; it was a hot pouch filled with sticky rice bought from the Chinese grocery store. It looked like astronaut food but it smelled like the back alley of Chinatown. To be honest, it was pretty delicious, but the sticky rice pouch definitely didn't help me look like a normal cool American kid. I badly wanted to find an identity so I could belong. *Is there a group for short kids? Is there a group for kids who used to play Ping-Pong?* And as much as I didn't want to be the foreign kid again . . . *Is there a group for foreign kids?*

An old but energetic Chinese art teacher in Beverly High named Po Lau hosted the school's Chinese Culture Club. It wasn't really a club with a mission statement; it was just a bunch of Chinese students gathering in Po Lau's classroom playing cards and video games at lunch. As much as I wanted to be American, the Chinese Culture Club became my lunchtime refuge. I hung out with Po Lau and the only three other Chinese kids in school, eating our weird Chinese lunches every day. It felt like visiting my uncle's house in Hong Kong. Po Lau would even heckle us with his terrible jokes in his thick Cantonese accent:

> "Hey, where is your playing cards?"
> "We are playing with them right now, Po."
> "You have the red cards and black cards, right?"
> "Yeah . . ."
> "But where is your green card?!"
> He folded over laughing at his own shitty punch line,
> while we shook our heads in embarrassment for him.

The Chinese Culture Club was a nice safety net, but it felt like a regression. I didn't want to spend the next four years of high school hibernating with three other Chinese kids inside of a dank classroom; I could have done that back in Hong Kong. I wanted to have the all-American high school adolescent experience. I wanted to play in the homecoming football game, I wanted to take a road trip in my dad's car and I wanted to go to prom with a white girl. I didn't care about hanging out with the cool kids, but I was tired of being the foreign kid. All I wanted to be was a "normal" American kid.

I met my first non-Chinese friend in Beverly Hills High during the second semester of freshman year. Jeremy was a Persian kid on the football team, but he didn't act particularly Persian or particularly like a football jock. We hit it off making fun of the other kids in our sixth-period computer class. Jeremy and his friends had a table on the top floor next to the cafeteria. And I started to sneak away from the Chinese Culture Club to hang out with them. They were the most diverse group of dudes I'd seen since the *We Are the World* music video. Jeremy and his cousin Phil Yadegari were Persians who were into normal American teenager stuff like *Star Wars*, *Madden* and the *Justice League*; Zaki Hashem was an honor student from Bangladesh; Bo Kim was a quiet Korean immigrant; Chris O'Connor was a tall, lanky half-white, half–Native American dude who wore T-shirts three sizes too big; and Derek Wah was an ABC (American-born Chinese) whose parents were also from Shanghai and he spoke Shanghainese. When a Shanghainese person finds another Shanghainese in America, it's like finding a best friend who has the same birthday and who also happens to be a long lost cousin.

It's an instant connection. The best part was that Derek and I could make fun of everyone else in Shanghainese. Derek, Jeremy, Phil, Zaki, Bo, Chris and I soon became best friends.

Nobody in this group fit into any particular high school archetype, and nobody cared to. This group of mish-moshed friends became my clique for the rest of my high school career. We weren't the coolest kids in school but we weren't nerds either. We didn't really care what others thought about us. I'd always pictured the American high school experience as a handsome, white high school quarterback scoring a game-winning touchdown at homecoming, then slow-dancing with the head cheerleader at the homecoming dance. But this diverse group of human beings from different backgrounds reflected an even more truthful version of America: a country of immigrants.

We never did anything cool like partying or underage drinking; we just threw around the football after school and played *Madden* at Phil's house. I had a hard curfew to go home for dinner every night. If I wasn't home by seven, my dad would call me and scream bloody murder in angry Shanghainese:

"Are you dead?!"

"No, I'm at Jeremy's house playing video games."

"If you're not dead, then why aren't you home for dinner?"

"I will come back later."

Then he'd switch gear to some classic Asian parent guilt-tripping. "Do you think I'm dead?"

"What? No."

"Then why do you disrespect your father like that?"

"Dad, I'll—"

"Come home for dinner now!" And he hung up.

I'm pretty sure these phone calls emotionally scarred me for life.

Most American kids would have probably rebelled and said, "Screw you, Dad! You're not the boss of me!" But I couldn't. Disrespecting your elders was the ultimate sin in Chinese culture. And most of all, I empathized with my dad. Mom was gone and my brother was in college; I was the only thread in our family that he could hang on to. I couldn't bear the burden of leaving my dad alone for dinner. As much as I wanted to hang out at Jeremy's house, I went home for dinner with my dad every night.

BET *RAP CITY*

Jeremy, Phil and Chris were big fans of rappers like 2Pac, Snoop Dogg and Bone Thugs-n-Harmony. I had never heard of any of those names before, and I felt left out whenever they talked about this hip-hop music. My dad always complained that rap music was too noisy and it sounded like "Buddhist monks reciting a poem." We grew up listening to Michael Jackson, Madonna and the Eagles. I knew nothing about hip-hop; I didn't even know 2Pac was dead. But I wanted to fit in with my friends, so I started consuming any hip-hop I could find. That's when I discovered BET.

BET stands for Black Entertainment Television; it is an American television network for the urban community. I later learned that *urban* is just another word for black people. BET featured urban TV series, urban music and urban gospel on Sundays. Tuning into BET was like opening Pandora's box to a whole new American world. I went from watching cartoons on Nickelodeon to studying *Rap City* on BET. I was mesmerized by the colorful hip-hop culture. Every day, rappers like 50 Cent would come on *Rap City* wearing XXXL basketball jerseys, with massive diamond chains on their necks, and count down the best urban music videos. Each music video was a portal into a whole new world that I'd never seen before. When I saw Jay-Z's *Big Pimpin'* music video for the first time, it changed my life. For those of you who don't remember *Big Pimpin'*, or are too white to be aware of it, *Big Pimpin'* was the greatest music video of all time. It featured hundreds of beautiful women in bikinis partying on a million-dollar yacht, as three rappers named Jay-Z, Bun B and Pimp C poured champagne on them for four minutes straight. And the girls were all loving it! My fifteen-year-old immigrant brain couldn't believe what I was seeing. *This is America? I'm fucking in! Big Pimpin'* was the epitome of the American dream and I needed to be part of it. I wanted to be like these larger-than-life American superheroes they called rappers. I wanted to be a pimp like Jay-Z and a gangster like 50 Cent. I made it my life's goal to live the *Big Pimpin'* lifestyle. Whenever I watched BET, I forgot I was a small foreign Chinese boy and I felt like a badass gangsta. I started imitating how the rappers walked and how they talked. I would go up to my classmates and say, "Yo what up, dog. Our geometry teacher is a bitch, homie." I learned how to speak proper American English from watching BET. I consumed at least three hours of music videos a day. These music videos were snippets of different versions of the American dream. They shaped my adolescence and they inspired me way beyond my high school years. Aside from *Big Pimpin'*, here are some of my favorite music videos that taught me about America.

TOP FIVE HIP-HOP MUSIC VIDEOS

1. Sisqó—*Thong Song.* "Baby! That thong thong thong thong thong!" This was one of the first songs I heard on American radio. It was catchy as hell, but I had no idea what a thong was. Then when I saw the music video, everything made sense. There was so much booty in that video that I almost slapped the TV. I didn't even know booty was a point of attraction on the opposite sex. Nobody had booties like that in Hong Kong. I learned what "thick" meant as a compliment, and I got a whole new appreciation for thick girls after watching this video.

2. Lil Jon & the Eastside Boyz—*Get Low.* "369 Damn She Fine!" This was America's introduction to crunk music. It was high-energy southern hip-hop with a sense of humor. I sang that every day in school. "Till all skeet skeet skeet skeet!" It took me a year to realize what skeet actually meant. This song was a quintessential soundtrack of my high school years. We even gave one girl in school the nickname "369" because, well . . . Damn she fine!

3. 50 Cent and Snoop Dogg—*P.I.M.P.* I didn't know what a pimp truly meant until I saw this music video. I looked it up in a dictionary and pimping seemed to be an illegal activity.

50 Cent and Snoop Dogg gave pimping a new meaning. They were strutting with their pimp canes, riding in a Rolls-Royce and dancing with the most beautiful girls. A P.I.M.P is simply a man who is living the American dream. Pimp became the ultimate compliment. Everybody wanted to be a pimp.

4. Big Tymers—*Still Fly*. Birdman and Mannie Fresh defined hood rich. This whole song was basically the dictionary description for hood rich. "Gator boots with my pimped out Gucci suits, ain't got no job, but I stay sharp." I might never understand that mentality to spend what you don't have, but it was awesome to see two ballers on a budget.

5. Nelly—*Country Grammar*. Nelly brought out the whole neighborhood in St. Louis in this video. There weren't any Rolls-Royces or yachts. It was hundreds of people dancing at a block party with Cadillacs and St. Louis BBQ. They looked like they were having more fun with nothing fancy at all. This was the American neighborhood party I wanted to be at. It was the hip-hop party I could relate to.

Another BET show that absolutely fascinated me was *Comicview*. It was an "urban" stand-up comedy showcase with "urban" stand-up comedians performing in front of an "urban" audience, talking about "urban" stereotypes. This was my first exposure to stand-up comedy. It was more than just funny to me; it was unrestrained, dynamic and culturally relevant. I couldn't really understand what the comedians were saying and I was lost on the stereotypes they were referring to. It was like a whole new language to me. I had no concept of the credit system in America, let alone the stereotype of black people having bad credit; I didn't understand why white people were always doing crazy things, like skydiving and hiking, that black people would never do; and I didn't understand what it meant when a comedian said, "Mama trippin'." Did his mom trip and fall over on the floor? Is she okay? Even though I couldn't understand half of the bits, I was enthralled by the performances. *Comicview* was a slice of real American culture that I'd never known before. I thought to myself, *If I can understand Comicview, I will understand everything about America.* So I watched BET *Comicview* religiously for three years. And I learned about this country from the realest American educators: comedians. They weren't just telling jokes, they were making insightful observations from a unique point of view. *Rap City* taught me American English; *Comicview* enlightened me about American culture. These shows had such a huge influence on my life. I soon found my first love in making hip-hop music before I eventually became a stand-up comedian.

I couldn't rap for shit, but I wanted so badly to be part of the glamorous rap game that I'd seen on *Rap City*. Chris downloaded a bootleg copy of Sony's ACID Music Studio, a beat-making software, and he started cranking out some sick beats. Then Jeremy, Phil and I would go to Chris's mom's apartment and record our raps on his five-dollar computer microphone. Next thing you know, we'd formed a rap group just like N.W.A. Chris's mom's apartment and his Dell desktop became our recording studio. We felt like the real deal and we called ourselves Syndakit. The first time I recorded at Chris's house, he played me a beat he had just made. It sounded like a real track I'd heard on *Rap City*. I pulled out my trigonometry notebook and I was ready to write my first rhymes, but I had no idea where to start.

    "So . . . what do I write?"

    "Just write anything you want." Chris was the Dr. Dre to my Eazy-E.

    "How much do I write?"

    "I think you need sixteen bars."

    I understood that "bars" were some kind of quantifier for lyrics and not Snickers, but is a bar one word? Is it a full sentence? Or can it be a fragment? Chris saw the confusion on my face, and he explained:

    "One bar is one line that is four beats."

    "Oh, yeah, totally, I got that."

I had no idea what a beat was. This was like one of those stupid dictionary descriptions where they explain a word with the same word you don't understand. *Pathological—of or relating to pathology.* If I knew what pathology meant I wouldn't have asked for the definition of pathology! But I went with it. I flipped past the trigonometry homework in my notebook, and started writing down my first sixteen bars.

Don't hate the player 'cause the player don't play, haters talk shit but the bullet stays.

And those were the first two bars I ever wrote. It was two uninspired, fraudulent lines copied from what I'd heard on BET. What bullet? I was an A student in Beverly Hills High School. I should have been rapping about the Pythagorean theorem. But I wanted to be a gangsta-ass rapper, so I rapped about sex, drugs and gangbanging. In reality, I was a virgin who had a seven o'clock curfew. I scribbled down another fourteen bars of garbage and I was ready to make my first gangsta rap song. Chris held up the five-dollar computer mic and I started spitting my sixteen bars. Two seconds in, Chris stopped me.

"What happened?" I was curious as to why he had stopped my incredible flow.

"You're not on beat."

"What do you mean I'm not on beat?"

I wasn't challenging him; I actually didn't know what being on beat meant.

"Jimmy, you have to rap to the rhythm of the music."

I had no idea that I was supposed to be matching the rhythm of the music. I was literally just talking over the music. When Chris played me the beat again, I mechanically bobbed my head to the kicks and snares, but I couldn't follow the tempo. And that's when I realized that this was exactly what the *Comicview* comedians meant when they said, "White people got no rhythm." This Chinese boy got no rhythm.

When the other kids were busy chasing girls and scoring booze, we went to Chris's house to make music. The thought of maybe getting on BET *Rap City* one day gave us something to strive for, but more importantly, making music gave us an identity. We weren't the random kids who hung out by the cafeteria anymore; we were now the kids who made hip-hop. We made

The Syndakit gang. Jeremy (top right), Phil (bottom right), Chris (bottom left). Throwing up random gang signs that we'd seen on BET. Needless to say, I never got laid in high school.

a full-length rap album with that five-dollar microphone and we pushed those CDs to everyone we knew in class. We'd burn the CDs and each carry a Walkman in class, showing people the songs. "Hey, check out our tracks, get it before we blow up. We gonna go platinum, homie." That was my sales pitch. I think we ended up selling three copies of the album for a total proceed of fifteen dollars, so technically we were only 499,997 records away from going platinum. We made just enough money to recoup for the five-dollar computer mic and a ten-dollar stack of CD-ROMs.

We even performed at the battle of the bands in our high school wearing ridiculous iron-on matching Syndakit T-shirts. Most people thought we were completely ridiculous, and rightfully so, but it was the first time anyone even noticed us. A skinny half-white guy, two Persian dudes and a Chinese immigrant rapping about gangster shit. We looked more like a sketch comedy group than a rap group.

Chris decided to take music more seriously, so he recruited two other friends from our school to our rap group who could actually rap: Yuji, a half-black, half-Japanese dude who acted like two black dudes, and Julian, a quietly cool black dude who was a great rapper. Jeremy, Phil and I would eventually get fazed out of Chris's songs, and rightfully so; we sucked. So I took matters into my own hands and downloaded a bootleg beat-making program called Fruity Loops and started to make my own beats. I came up with a producer name, Doc West. An uninspired attempt to combine my two favorite hip-hop producers' names, Dr. Dre and Kanye West. I sat in front of my computer for four hours a day in an attempt to come up with something decent. Then in an ultimate coup d'état, I recruited Julian and Yuji to join my own rap group. The three of us would be a perfect balance of 1.5 Asian guys and 1.5 black guys. I named our rap group the

YELLOW PANTHERS

In hindsight, I'm very surprised nobody beat me up for coming up with that name. I guess I have always been more of a comedian than a musician. Yellow Panthers forever!

I was the worst rapper alive; I didn't even have the concept of a bar or a beat. That's like a car mechanic who has never heard of an engine or a transmission. I wanted to live the rapper lifestyle, but I didn't know the first thing about rap. I wasn't an artist; I was a fraud. But in the process of struggling to stay on beat, I discovered my first creative outlet. It didn't matter if our songs were going to make it on the Billboard Hot 100 Chart; we felt like we were making something of ourselves. With bootleg software, a five-dollar microphone, and some shitty lyrics, we made something out of nothing. Best of all, we didn't need permission to make this. There were no rules. It felt like the opposite of everything I had to follow in school and in my family. I smelled the independent spirit of hip-hop: it smelled like America, which I guess happened to smell like the fumes coming out of an old Dell computer. For the first time, I felt like I was freely frolicking in the streets without parental supervision like an American kid.

TOO COOL FOR PROM, BUT NOT REALLY

I never got a record deal, but I experienced creative freedom for the first time. I still was nowhere close to being popular. I never went to any fancy Beverly Hills High School house parties, I never smoked weed in front of the swim gym and I never went to prom. Not that I didn't want to do those things; I never got invited to them. I spent the rest of my high school career holding on to the music; it was the only thing that kept me from being a complete loser.

I wanted to go to prom with a high school sweetheart. I mean who wouldn't? But I had no date in sight, so I just said fuck it and pretended to be a cool antisocial kid who didn't care about prom. A part of me felt like I was missing out in life, but the other part convinced myself, *Who cares? You were never trying to fit in anyways. Own the coolness of being a rebel badass who don't give a shit about prom.* I remember the night everyone else went to prom. I was just sitting at home watching *MADtv* with my dad. We loved that show and we've always preferred it over *SNL*. My dad always got very excited when the hilarious Bobby Lee came on-screen; any Asian person who made it on American television was a big deal. At that time, it was just Bobby Lee and Yao Ming. That night, my dad never asked me, "Hey, why aren't you going to prom?" He didn't even know what prom was. If he did know about it, he'd probably call it stupid American bullshit, especially if he found out how much money he'd have to fork out for my tux rental.

The only person that ever pressured me to go to prom was Phil's mom, a nice Persian woman named Fariba. During my senior year, every time I went over to Phil's house, Fariba would say to me:

"Jimmy, you have to go to prom, it's a once in a lifetime experience!"

"Fariba, it's okay, I don't want to spend the money."
I didn't want to tell her the actual reason was I didn't have a date in sight.

"Jimmy Joon [Joon is an endearing term you put after someone's name in Farsi], I'll pay the money, you have to go, or you will regret it your whole life." An all-expenses-paid prom still doesn't sound that great if you don't have a date.

"Fariba Joon," I jokingly responded, "nemi khom," which is Farsi for "I don't want." I fended Fariba off for the rest of the year with the Farsi phrases I picked up from hanging out with my Persian friends, which was the official second language of Beverly Hills High School.

Maybe I'm still in denial, but I never regretted not going to prom. One thing I really did want to do in high school was to join the football team. I wanted to live the all-American dream of scoring a touchdown under the Friday night lights and spiking the ball in the end zone. I was pretty fast and had some actual ball skills; my dream was to play kick return like my hero Dante Hall. He was a five-foot-six kick return specialist who played for the Kansas City Chiefs. He weaved and juked defensive players twice his size and scored hundred-yard touchdowns without ever getting touched. I was also five-foot-six and I thought I could be like Dante. So I went to my dad and asked him to sign the waiver for me to play football. He never even considered it for a moment; he just laughed right in my face.

"You? Football? Come on."
"But, Dad, I'm fast and—"
"I'm not signing a paper that'll make you die."

And he was probably right. I was a hundred pounds soaking wet. I would have gotten concussed just sitting on the bench. My body was never destined to play anything more than a serious game of Ping-Pong.

I eventually graduated high school as a bona fide virgin with a 3.9 GPA. People might have remembered me as the ridiculous rapper kid who watched too much BET, but I was no longer the weird foreign kid. I never got to slow-dance with my lover at prom or play football at homecoming, but I had an authentic American high school experience. I found a group of friends who came from every part of the world and we bonded over Jay-Z. To me, that is more American than scoring a touchdown at homecoming.

THE PINNACLE OF MY MUSIC CAREER

Years later, when I was in college, I hit the pinnacle of my music career. I received a phone call from an unknown number. I picked up the phone and a man with a gravelly voice asked:

"Are you Doc West?"

"Yes, that's me." I was ecstatic that it was a call for hip-hop producer Doc West, not Jimmy.

"That's great. I heard your beats online, I love them."

Is this a dream? "Thank you, sir."

Then he introduced himself. "My name is Laronn James."

"Excuse me? YOU are Lebron James!?" I almost shitted myself.

"No, it's LaRONN James."

"Oh, okay. Sorry, nice to meet you, Laronn."

"Are you, by any chance, a religious person?"

"Hmm, no, not really."

"You're not a serious Christian or anything?"

"No, I'm not religious. Why?"

Well, this is probably a Jehovah's Witness guy, complimenting my beats to lure me into their religion. I should have known it was too good to be true.

"Okay, that's great," Laronn continued, "because religious people don't agree with my line of work."

Ah, drug dealer, cool. As long as he wanted to buy some of my beats, I didn't care if he sold crack to babies. I don't judge.

"I'm in the adult entertainment business." Laronn dropped the bomb. "I make porn, and I perform in it." I wasn't sure how to feel about that, a bit impressed I guess; I quietly nodded. "Oh, that's cool" was my only response.

Laronn started opening up and talked with more excitement. "I love your beats, man. I want to buy a couple of them to put in my movies."

"Yeah, for sure. That'll be cool." I knew this was a story I'd be able to tell for the rest of my life.

"That's great, I want to put one of your beats in a new trailer for my website. It's called Fudgestick.com. Check it out when you get a chance."

And I indeed went and checked out Fudgestick.com, for research purposes. The name was pretty on the nose; it was Laronn and his massive fudgestick having sex with MILFs. (If you don't know what that means, look it up when you're alone.) Two weeks later, my beat was on the front page of Fudgestick.com, accompanying Laronn's performance in a hardcore porno trailer. With Laronn's purchase of my beat, I officially became a professional musician, and I guess also a professional pornographer. This was the pinnacle of my music career, the highlight of my life. Fudge-stick.com wrote me my first paycheck in show business.

PS: Sadly, Fudgestick.com is no longer operating. I checked, for re-search purposes. Maybe I'll show the world my Fudgestick.com music video trailer on The Tonight Show someday.

CHAPTER FOUR

HOW TO GET HIGH

For Asian kids, going to college is like going to elementary school. It's mandatory. Asian parents are never proud of you for going to college; they are just not disappointed.

"Dad, I got into college!"
"So? Your cousin has three PhDs, from Harvard."

Both my first and second college choices were in Los Angeles: UCLA and USC. And they both unequivocally rejected me. I had good grades but I didn't have enough extracurricular activities because apparently, the Yellow Panthers wasn't a legitimate activity to these highbrowed admission officers; maybe I should have included Fudgestick.com on my college application. I *was* accepted by UC San Diego, the San Diego sister school of UCLA. I thought that was basically UCLA by the beach, so I went in blind without even visiting the campus. People used to always tell me, "College is the best four years of your life, enjoy it!" That's way too much pressure. And that's saying after you graduate college, everything is downhill from there. What a morbid thought. Not only was it not the best four years of my life, it turned out to be the worst five years of my life.

I hated the school part of college and I despised the social part of UCSD. There was zero school spirit in UCSD. Our mascot was called the Triton; it's a naked old man holding up a fork. Our sports teams all sucked; there were no Division I teams other than water polo, fencing and men's volleyball. UCSD focused on academics and sports that nobody cared about. While my brother was partying at the UCLA versus USC rivalry football games at the Rose Bowl with a hundred thousand people, I was watching the Triton's men's volleyball team. The only cool thing in UCSD was its proximity to the beach and the surfing culture in San Diego, but I could barely swim. When my dad took me to the beach in Hong Kong when I was three, I cried and begged him not to put me near the water. I was born to be a land dweller. I ended up spending the better part of my college career smoking weed to mentally escape from UCSD.

UCSD's student body was made up of a majority of Asian students. I was one of them, but I didn't want to be lumped in with everyone else. I was used to being different. So I tried my hardest to be the opposite of a stereotypical Asian student: I grew my hair out down to my shoulders, I started smoking weed and I never went to class: the holy trinity of an underachieving party kid from Arizona State. The only difference is, I wasn't getting laid. I wasn't trying to be a bad boy; it was a cry for help to stand out in a school with twenty thousand students. I felt like my identity was being judged based on the other Asians around me instead of my own personality, my inside voice screamed, *I listen to Jay-Z, motherfuckers!* In high school, I didn't want to be perceived as the weird foreign kid; in college, I didn't want to be perceived as the same as everyone else. I had a new identity crisis. One way to not be another Asian is to smoke so much weed that you transcend into being a stoner. If someone asked, "Hey, do you know that kid Jimmy from dorm 706?" I wanted people to say, "Yeah, the kid who's high all the time?" instead of "Oh yeah, that Asian kid."

I went into UC San Diego as a mechanical engineering major but I was smoking way too much weed to keep up with the engineering curriculum. At the highness that I was, it would have taken me seventeen years to graduate with an engineering degree. I had no idea what I wanted to do. So I switched my major to economics, the easiest major that Asian parents would still approve of. I didn't give a shit about the economy. How was I supposed to care about fiscal policies when I only had student loan debts and no assets? As long as weed was twenty bucks a gram, the Federal Reserve was doing their job. I ended up graduating UCSD after five long years with a pathetic 2.7 GPA. I Daniel Day-Lewis'd myself into being a stoner who didn't care about grades, and at some point I actually started to believe I was this stoner character. There's a Chinese saying that describes when someone goes too deep into something and they lose themselves in it, 走火入魔, which literally translates to "the fire leaves and the devil enters." In my case it was "the brain leaves and the THC enters."

HOW TO GET DEPORTED

Tijuana is a Mexican border town just south of San Diego where all the underage college kids in San Diego go to party. It's a dirty cesspool of sins, which translates to a Disneyland for college students. There are dance clubs, strip clubs, clubs with donkeys, cocaine, sex and everything a college student could dream of. In my freshman year at UCSD, my dorm mate, John, and I went on our first trip to Tijuana with our friend Ian. Ian grew up in San Diego and had been going to Tijuana since high school, and he knew all the party spots. He was like our gringo Gandalf of Tijuana.

We got off the San Diego city trolley around 10 P.M., ready for some shenanigans. We walked over the border and took a Mexican taxi to Revolution Boulevard, where all the debaucheries go down. It was a street filled with dance clubs and strip clubs with neon lights, accented by the smell of tacos and used condoms. Right as we got off the cab, a shady Mexican man wearing a cheap suit and sunglasses approached us. "Titties?" He motioned his hands like two titties bouncing on his chest. Of course we stopped and listened. He repeated, "Titties? Titty bar?" As intriguing as that sounded, our plan was to go to the nightclub first. So we politely declined and kept walking. He followed us down the street and kept on pushing. "Titties? Sucky sucky? Fucky fucky?" He was getting shadier by each word. "Titties? Titties? Cocaine? Heroin?" It escalated quickly. As he finally gave up, he just yelled out, *"Maricon!"* Within the first thirty seconds of arriving in Tijuana, we were offered titties, blow jobs and cocaine; us three *Maricons* knew we were in for a wild night.

Ian led us to a dance club on Revolution Boulevard. It was twenty dollars for an all-you-can-drink dance club party. We treated that bar like starving refugees at HomeTown Buffet. Next thing I knew, we were hammered, fist-pumping in the middle of a sweaty Mexican dance club, and John was nowhere to be found. "Shit, he probably went to the titty bar by himself," I said to Ian. Then we heard the crowd cheering on the other side of the club, and we saw John in the middle of the commotion; he was dancing like Beyoncé as water was pouring onto his head from the upstairs balcony. John was having the time of his life. Ian and I looked up and we realized it wasn't water being poured on John; it was actually a dude pissing onto John's head from upstairs. John was way too drunk to realize he had been christened in a Mexican golden shower.

"No way." I looked at Ian in disbelief. "We have to get him out of there." "John!" Ian screamed out. "Come on, let's go!" John was more excited than I'd ever seen him. "Guys, this is amazing!" Ian and I looked at each other, not sure what to say. John yelled from across the club, "They are pouring water on me and the whole crowd is going crazy! This is awesome!" We just nodded and let him have it; it would be better if he never found out, and I hope he never reads this book.

When we finally got out of the club; all the hustlers, drug dealers and prostitutes flocked to us like a pack of vultures. We ducked into this hole-in-the-wall taco shop to calm down from the overstimulation. We sat down on the high stools with a couple Dos Equises in front of the hot iron skillet filled with taco meat. The chubby Mexican lady with a red apron started heating up the little corn tortillas. She masterfully scooped a spoonful of meat, sprinkled a garnish of onion and cilantro and flipped the tacos onto a plate right in front of our drooling mouths. I was skeptical about the corn tortillas at first, from what my grandpa taught me in El Pollo Loco: it's flour or nothing. So I asked the lady, "Do you have flour tortillas?" She didn't even bother to look at me. Ian, a Tijuana taco shop veteran, said, "Dude, nobody does flour tortillas here; you sound like an idiot gringo. Eat the corn ones, they're delicious." I reluctantly bit into the corn-wrapped *carne asada* taco, and I realized I had been living a lie. This corn tortilla tasted like Salma Hayek's lips. The sweet corn taste and the grainy texture layered with the meat, onion and cilantro transported me to a Mexican nirvana. I wanted to cry and hug the chubby Mexican lady who made this perfect taco. But I was a little bit too drunk to stand up straight. We decided we'd had enough excitement for one night and it'd probably be a good idea to head back to San Diego before another golden shower hit us. So we called a cab back to the border, but this wasn't where this story ended; it was where it began.

Going into Mexico from the United States was a wide-open revolving door with almost no security. Crossing the border from Mexico to the United States was quite the opposite. The border crossing point was a gray windowless cement tunnel with metal barriers. Instead of wide-open revolving doors, there were border patrol agents with guards carrying assault rifles standing behind them. This was no place to fuck around. I was a bit worried because we were all pretty drunk and John smelled like pee. We tried blinking really hard a few times to sober ourselves up, a drunkard's futile attempt at sobriety. Ian, our trusted Tijuana guru, explained to me: "Dude, don't worry, it's super easy. I just show them my driver's license and tell them I'm an American citizen, they let me right in every time. No questions asked." Ian went up to the border patrol. And he was right; he got right through. Then John stumbled up to the border patrol counter, and he went through in a breeze. If they let John through, I was pretty sure I was in good shape. The stern border patrol lady signaled me over, and I promptly handed her my California driver's license. She scanned my license.

"Are you an American citizen?"
"Yes."

I replied exactly how Ian had told me. Except I was too drunk to remember one minor detail: **I wasn't an American citizen**. Unlike Ian, I was a permanent resident with a green card. Oops.

The agent typed something into her computer and she stopped. She studied me for a long beat; then without saying a word, she got up and whispered something to the armed guard next to her. The guard looked square into my soul and marched two steps towards me. "Come with me, sir."

The man with the assault rifle led me down a long empty concrete tunnel to a small empty room. It had a wooden desk, two metal chairs and a blinding LED light on the ceiling. He stood in one corner with both of his hands holding the assault rifle. He said, "Have a seat." I sat down on the cold metal folding chair in front of a heavy wooden desk. I sat there for thirty minutes and the guard never took his eyes off of me. Finally, the border agent who had checked my ID entered the room. She shut the door behind her and sat down across from me. She cut to the chase:

"So why did you lie?"

"I . . . I don't . . ." I was so nervous I could barely form a sentence.

"Why did you lie about being an American citizen?"

"I'm sorry, that's what my friend told me to say. I'm so sorry."

"Your friend told you to lie?"

"No, but he said he just shows his driver's license and says he's an American citizen, and he told me to do the same."

"Well, is he an American citizen?"

"Yes."

"Well, are you?"

"No."

She looked over to the guard and had no further questions. I pleaded:

"I'm so sorry. I didn't mean to lie. I just didn't think about it. I was going out in Tijuana and I was a bit drunk. I just did what my friend said he does when he crosses the border. I'm so sorry, ma'am. I'm just a stupid college student."

She didn't respond; she got up and exited the room. Leaving me alone once again with the armed guard. This time, I was sure I was going to get executed by his assault rifle.

Another thirty minutes passed by, and surprisingly, I was still alive. I had lost all hope of ever seeing any of my family and friends in the United States. I was contemplating my last words. I thought about where I'd live when I got deported, where I'd go to school and how I would survive on my own in Hong Kong, China or wherever they were going to send me. Maybe they were calling me an Uber to Guantanamo Bay. But mostly, I thought about how disappointed my parents would be in their idiot son, who got drunk in Tijuana and lied to a border patrol agent. Then the door swung open and the border patrol lady came in again, holding a stack of paperwork. This time, she was accompanied by two other border patrol agents: a Latino man and a middle-aged Asian man. I was ready for them to seal my fate as all three of them looked at me with utter disappointment. The lady put the paperwork in front of me and said to me:

"You are lucky this time. I am going to put down that you forgot your green card, and we won't charge you with anything or put anything on your record."

The gods took mercy on me; I lived to American another day.

Then the Latino agent said, "There is a fee for not having your green card at the border. Pay that and you can go."

I looked down at the paperwork; the fee was $360, basically my entire college checking account. *Hey, can you guys just deport me instead?* But I had sobered up enough to know that this was one of the best deals I'd ever get in my life. I gladly paid the fee and thanked the lady for her mercy. As the guard ushered me out of the room, the Asian border patrol officer said one last thing to me that I'll never forget:

"Don't do that again, or we'll send you back to where you came from."

Those words shook me to my bones. I felt like the lost thirteen-year-old foreigner again. All the Pledge of Allegiances, American football and BET *Rap City* didn't change anything; I was still just a foreigner living in America. And worst of all, this came from an Asian American person. I was angry. I was angry that an Asian brother sold me out. I was angry that he thought he was better than me. I was angry that no matter how hard I tried, I was still a foreigner. I couldn't come up with a response that wouldn't send me to prison. I just took the comment and silently walked out. I was still nothing more than an immigrant who could be deported at any time.

A YOUNG STONER LIVING IN A RETIREMENT COMMUNITY

I was depressed when I went home that summer after freshman year. I was back at square one of my immigrant journey, and

I had learned nothing in school other than how to roll a joint. I stayed with my dad, who had moved into a retirement community in Monterey Park filled with old Chinese people. I was a longhaired college boy living in a sixty-five-and-older apartment complex. People looked at me like I was some kind of alien invading their morning tai chi class. I tried being friendly with our neighbors but they weren't having it. I greeted our eighty-year-old Chinese neighbor with a warm smile. "Hi, how are you?" No response; he just stared at me. I tried again in Mandarin. *"Ni hao."* Still no response; he judgmentally looked me up and down and walked away. It was going to be a bleak summer.

There was a community bench right outside of my bedroom. Every day at 7:00 A.M., I would wake up to old ladies chatting in Mandarin. An old lady said to her friend:

"When did you stop getting your period?"
"I was thirty-nine, it was early," her friend responded in a matter-of-fact manner.
"I stopped getting mine when I was fifty-four."
And that was the day I learned about menopause.

I didn't have a car and all my friends from Beverly Hills High lived twenty miles away. I went from the general population in college to solitary confinement in a Chinese retirement community. I felt like I was trapped on a leper island quarantined from the world. I would go down to the park across from the apartment and sit alone on a bench just to get away from the grandmas talking about their periods. One day, as if it was a sign from God, a Latino kid riding a BMX bicycle stopped by the bench I was sitting on. "Yo, you smoke weed?" he asked me. My long hair signaled for weed dealers like the bat signal called for Batman. I said, "Yeah. You got some?" And he pulled out a joint. "You smoke chewy?" I had no idea what chewy meant, but any weed would do at this point. "Sure." And we lit up the joint right there in the park. After a couple of hits, I started coughing like a real amateur.

"Oh man, this is strong."
"You never smoked chewy before, huh?"
"No, I don't think so. What is it?"
"It's weed with cocaine sprinkled on it."

My eyes went wide. I'm sure it was a combination of shock and the cocaine coursing down my bloodstream. He made cocaine sound like an ice cream topping. I had never done coke before, and I'd just smoked it in a joint with a random dude on a bicycle in a park across from my dad's retiree apartment. I panicked. "I got to go." I got up and speed-walked home in an effort to sober up. I couldn't throw up something I'd smoked, and I couldn't water it down either, so I just lay in my bed with my heart pounding faster than Floyd Mayweather hitting a speed bag.

I didn't know what a panic attack was at the time; I thought I was having a full-blown heart attack. My dad was watching TV in his bedroom, no idea his son just smoked a cocaine-laced joint. I had a decision to make. *Should I wait it out and hope my heart doesn't blow out of my chest? Or should I tell my dad I did some cocaine so he can take me to the hospital?* The first choice could mean death; the second choice would come with a lifetime of shame. As a proper Asian, I chose death over shame. I hopped into the shower to try to calm myself down. I took a forty-five-minute shower, twice, and my heart was still jumping out of my throat. I lay down on the couch and turned on *SportsCenter* on ESPN. The familiar voices of Stan Verrett and Neil Everett eased my panic and I started to dose off. I gave myself a fifty-fifty chance of waking up, scared to my core that I'd sleep forever. When I did manage to wake up the next morning, I wasn't sure if I was still living or I had gone to hell where the TV is permanently stuck on ESPN. Actually, I could argue that'd be heaven for me.

I started praying to Jesus after this near-death experience. "Lord, thank you for saving me from smoking chewy—that's a joint laced with cocaine, in case you've never heard of that." I felt my life going down an even steeper spiral. When I went back to school, I spent most of my sophomore year locked inside of my room, trying to not die again. I needed to do something drastic to snap out of this slump.

FOREIGN FOREIGN EXCHANGE STUDENT

In my junior year at UCSD, I moved into an apartment in San Diego with my high school friends, Phil from the lunch table, who also went to UCSD, and our mutual friend Bobby, who also went to Beverly Hills High School. Bobby's specialty was peer pressure. Whenever I didn't want to go out with him, he'd put on a full-court press. "Come on, Jimmy, don't be a pussy. Jimmy, come on, man, why are you being like that?" And he wouldn't stop until I went with him. It was annoying at times, but I desperately needed someone like Bobby to pull me out of my funk. One day, Bobby threw out a grandiose idea:

"Jimmy, let's go study abroad in Italy."

"What? No way. Studying abroad is for rich white girls, I can't afford to go to Italy." Really, I didn't want to go because I was scared of yet another change. Since I moved to America, my whole life had been a study-abroad trip.

"Come on, Jimmy, why are you being like that? We are going to go to Italy and drink wine, eat pasta and hang out with hot Italian girls. Jimmy, come on, don't be a pussy."

A month later, I was sitting on a plane next to Bobby on the way to Italy. I took out an extra twenty thousand dollars in student loans and we spent the next semester in Florence.

It was yet another new start for me. The great thing about studying abroad was that I wasn't the only foreign kid; everyone was the foreign kid. While everyone tried to get used to the new country, I'd already had a master class in assimilation. Bobby and I shared an apartment with a group of fellow study-abroad students from all over the States. Tim was a fashionable gay man from Florida; Nick was a straightforward New Yorker; Josh was a streetwise chef from Wisconsin; and Alex was a half-Korean, half-white hippie from San Francisco. It was like a season of *The Real World* minus the hot tub. We were all from different parts of

America, but we all felt like foreigners in Italy. While everyone felt like a fish out of water, I felt right in my element.

The Italians were not as politically correct as people in America. I passed by the Florentine flea market when I walked back to our apartment every day. The merchants peddled everything from overpriced truffle oil to miniature souvenir statues of David. It was a tourist trap and I looked like an easy target. Every time I walked by the market, the Italian merchants would greet me with three different greetings from three different Asian languages. *"Konichiwa!" "Ni hao!" "Annyeong!"* But they'd never just say, "Hi, how are you?" in English. Then I'd turn to the merchants and say, "Yeah, good day to you too, sir." One merchant continued the charade with a bow and said, *"Xie xie."* I wanted to respond, *"Xie xie* to your *madre,* bitch." But I restrained myself. Even though I was an American student who spoke better English than them, they still insisted I was a Chinese tourist.

Aside from a few *konichiwas* from ignorant merchants, studying abroad was an absolutely amazing life-changing experience. I took classes that were barely classes. I had a wine-tasting class where we got drunk on high-end wine every week; a food critique class where our homework was to eat at amazing restaurants and write about it; an architecture class where we browsed the historical Florentine sites like tourists; and a class called History of the Mafia. Yes, that was the real name of a real class, where we literally watched *The Godfather: Part II* with our ex-mafioso teacher. It was more like a summer camp than school. None of these credits transferred back to my economics degree in UCSD, but who cares? I was having the time of my life. I forgot about my near-death chewy experience and my near-deportation episode in Tijuana. Every weekend we'd visit a different city or a different country: Rome, Milan, Amsterdam, Dublin or Barcelona. We partied at the coolest Italian nightclubs and smoked hash in front of the Santa Croce church; being sacrilegious never felt so good. It was exactly what I needed to break out of my funk. I felt the world had finally opened up and I was no longer trapped under my Chinese family rules, my boring college curriculum and the confines of a dreadful retirement home. It was the first time I felt the freedom of being an American, and I had to go to Italy to find it.

When I came home to the States, I felt like I was coming to America for the first time again. I'd forgotten how wide the streets were in California, and I'd forgotten how to dress like a Californian. Everyone was driving down the Pacific Coast Highway wearing T-shirts and sandals, and I was trying to walk three miles to the grocery store rocking an Italian blazer. The study-abroad trip was such an amazing experience; it raised the bar for my standard of living. It made me not ever want to go back to my inadequate life back home. I felt a purposeful depression. I wasn't sad; I was unsatisfied. I wanted more out of life. I needed to step my life up.

THE *BEAVIS AND BUTT-HEAD* GUY

The college graduation ceremony felt more like a deadline than a celebration. It marked the day when I'd go from being a student to officially becoming an unemployed adult. After my trip to Florence, I didn't want to settle for any mundane job like I settled for a mundane college experience. *But what should I do with my life? How am I supposed to find a job if I don't even know what I want to do?* I didn't want to go to my graduation ceremony. And I was also very hung over from the night before when I tried to drink my problems away. I planned to pop Advils and watch *SportsCenter* in my bed all day, and then of course, Bobby gave me no choice.

"Hey, dude, let's go to the graduation together."

"Nah, I can't sit in the sun for four hours with a hangover."

"Come on, Jimmy, don't be a pussy. The guy from *Beavis and Butt-Head* is going to be the commencement speaker. It's going to be awesome."

"The *Beavis and Butt-Head* guy?"

The *Beavis and Butt-Head* guy was, of course, Mike Judge, the man who created *Beavis and Butt-Head, King of the Hill, Office Space,* and the man who'd eventually create an HBO show called *Silicon Valley.*

I watched *Beavis and Butt-Head* when I first came to America. Even though I didn't have a strong grasp on the English language yet, it made me laugh out loud with the way it was drawn and its weird sayings. I had no idea what Cornholio meant, but "I am Cornholio, I need teepee for my bunghole" was absolutely hilarious. *Beavis and Butt-Head* and *The Simpsons* were the only shows I watched that weren't on BET.

I didn't think anybody cool ever graduated from UCSD. So I dragged my ass to the graduation ceremony with a pounding headache. Our chancellor, Marye Anne Fox, kicked off the commencement ceremony with a quote: "It was the best of times, it was the worst of times. It was the age of wisdom, it was the age of foolishness." It was the lamest quote from *A Tale of Two Cities* by Charles Dickens. I immediately started to regret coming to this ceremony.

She droned on for another five minutes with generic "inspirational" remarks, and it felt like two hours with my massive hangover. Finally, they introduced Mike Judge. Mike looked way different than I had imagined. He was an athletic middle-aged dude with a sleekly shaved head, dressed in a polished black suit. He looked more like Jason Statham in *The Transporter* than the guy who drew *Beavis and Butt-Head*. He came up to the microphone in front of a thousand graduating students. "Ahh-huhuhuhu." He opened with the classic Butt-Head noise and continued in Beavis's voice. "Graduating class of 2009, hee-hee-hee." Then he switched gears to the familiar Hank Hill voice. "Boy, I tell you what, Class of 2009. It is indeed my pleasure to be with you this afternoon." Then Boomhauer came to life. "The dang ol' Chancellor Fox, man, the dang ol' thank you very much." The crowd lit up and I forgot I had a hangover.

Mike talked about how he graduated UCSD with a physics degree because that's what everyone said he should do. "Our high school guidance counselor and adults in general had us all convinced that if we just got a degree in science, jobs would just come raining out of the sky." He had always wanted to do comedy but didn't think it was really possible. After graduating, he settled for a job in Silicon Valley, during the original tech boom in the eighties. He soon realized he couldn't deal with the cultish, overachieving culture in that world, so he quit and became a touring musician. He was just as lost as I was. He then stumbled into an animation studio, and finally saw his dream of doing comedy materializing as a possibility. "For the first time, I was motivated. I was a man on a mission," Mike said in his speech. Shortly after, *Beavis and Butt-Head* was born, and the rest was history. He left the job that everyone told him he should do to become one of the most successful comedic voices in America.

That speech spoke to my lost, hungover college self. I couldn't imagine wasting my life away at a job based on an economics degree I never cared for, but I was too afraid to find my passion. I could hear my dad saying, "Doing what you love is how you become homeless." Finding a passion seemed as unrealistic as the Yellow Panthers winning a Grammy. Mike's commencement speech gave me the permission that my parents never gave me; it gave me the permission to quit what others thought I should do and find something I was truly passionate about. I wanted to find the thing that made me tick. And when I eventually stumbled into a comedy club, I felt that feeling of stumbling into the animation studio he described in his speech, and I knew I'd found *that thing* I was passionate about. And as fate would have it, Mike Judge would be the one who gave me my first big break in pursuing what I loved. Mike cast me on *Silicon Valley* five years after that commencement speech, not knowing I was sitting in the audience that day.

Pursue what you love, not what you should.

CHAPTER FIVE

HOW TO
STAND UP

My dad had set me up with an internship at Smith Barney, a prestigious financial consulting firm his friend worked at. I interned at their ritzy Beverly Hills office under one of their top financial advisers; it was the internship every parent dreamed of for their kid. I felt like a baller; I reconciled tax documents for their millionaire clients, I did analysis on mutual funds and my boss handled Kevin Sorbo's finances, a.k.a. Hercules. I thought that was the coolest thing ever. Needless to say,

I hadn't met a lot of celebrities before then and I was easily impressed. I had a blast during the first few weeks of the internship, daydreaming about a successful future that my dad would be so proud of. But after a month at that office, the routine set in and an intense dread of being stuck behind a desk for the rest of my life came over me. *Am I really going to be reconciling Kevin Sorbo's taxes for the rest of my life?* That became a recurring nightmare of mine; in the dream, I would be crunching numbers on an old Dell desktop and Hercules would come up behind me and crack me with his whip. "Faster, you mortal!" Then I'd cry to the image of his diversified mutual fund portfolio.

I started to hate everything about the internship, and I couldn't wait until my three-month sentence was over. I hated mutual funds, I hated CNBC and I hated Hercules. But at the same time, I knew how proud my dad was of his son who was following in his footsteps to become a financial adviser. He'd ask me with a sweet sense of pride on his face: "How's the internship going?" "It's going great! Today we worked on a couple Vanguard funds." I said it with a fake stapled grin on my stupid face. I didn't have the heart to tell him I hated the internship and I thought Vanguard funds were fucking stupid.

During my last week of the internship, Dad delivered some breaking news: "Jimmy! My friend at Smith Barney said he wants to offer you a full-time job when you graduate! Congratulations!" I'd never seen him so excited. I'm sure this was one of the happiest moments of his life, but in contrast, this was one of the most dismal moments of my life. Tears of joy almost rolled down from his eyes, while tears of absolute sadness almost poured down from mine. "Oh . . . that's great." I uttered those words like a zombie. The thought of looking at mutual funds for one more day, let alone for the rest of my life, made me feel dead inside. I felt like I was stuck in a terrible relationship, and I didn't know how to break up with my girlfriend who thought everything was going perfectly. Dad wanted to go out for dinner that night to celebrate.

"Where do you want to go? Anywhere you want."

"Dad, listen . . ." There was no way to let him down easily; I just had to do it. "I don't want to work for Smith Barney."

The joy disappeared from his face. He was in shock. He was in denial. He was blindsided. He asked me a question that he prayed I'd say yes to: "Do you have another job?"

"No." I couldn't even make eye contact with him.

He walked away, mourning the loss of his son that night.

I went from a dream internship to becoming every parent's worst nightmare. My dad thought I was delusional. He was too disappointed to ever confront me face to face, so he tried to passive aggressively get me back on track by sending me emails from CareerBuilder.com. "Jimmy, did you check your email today?" He'd say it in a deep, emotionless tone, making sure that I sensed his disappointment. "No, not yet." "Check it, I sent you three links from CareerBuilder.com. Real people are hiring." And this happened for years to come. I couldn't imagine the torment I put my dad through during those years. It was probably like having a son hooked on heroin, and he sent me CareerBuilder.com job leads instead of rehab brochures. To his credit, he never gave up on me. One could argue that not taking a "legit" job in order to find my passion was one of the stupidest decisions in my life, or now in hindsight, you could say that I was brave for making such a risky decision; but for me it wasn't even a decision. Taking a chance was the only way I could live with myself. I'd rather take a chance and fail miserably than to have never tried at all.

LOWBALL JIM

"What made you get into stand-up comedy?" Many people have asked me that question, and I can never give them a rosy answer that'd satisfy them. I've heard other comedians answer that question with a beautiful life story. "I used to sneak into the movie theater and watch Eddie Murphy's *RAW* with my brother and it changed my life. From that day on, my only goal in life was to become a stand-up comedian." And "The day my brother passed away with a congenital heart disease, I went onstage to my very first open mic." Beautiful, but who gives a shit? I'm not afraid to disappoint people and answer the question with the simple truth.

> "So what made you get into stand-up comedy?"
> "*I was fucking desperate.*"

I was twenty-one years old when I did my first open mic. Twenty-one was supposed to be the prime of my life where I partied every night, did Ecstasy and had unadulterated sex with hot strangers. Instead, I was stewing away in my dad's apartment playing *Madden* with Phil during my last summer vacation from college. I couldn't accept this as my reality, especially after coming back from Florence. Phil's an awesome dude but the thought of playing PlayStation in my dad's apartment for the rest of my life gave me an anxiety attack. I wanted to party like Mike "The Situation" on *Jersey Shore. I wanted to live!*

I needed to expand my horizon and find a community of friends. So I decided to sign up for a Brazilian jujitsu class because I was a fan of the UFC, but I totally forgot people actively try to break each other's arms in this sport. In my very first jujitsu class, the Brazilian instructor mounted on top of me and demonstrated a guillotine choke in front of the class. Before I could tap out in submission, the front of my esophagus was pressed against the back of my spine and I almost passed out. I thought he had cracked my windpipe; luckily I only had a sore throat for two weeks. People always tell you, "Never give up. Don't be a quitter." Those people have never gotten choked by a Brazilian jujitsu black belt. I should have quit halfway through day one, but like a good idiot who believed in old idioms, I stuck with it for three painful months.

They would always team me up with the girls during sparring exercises because I was the smallest guy in class. *What's the fun in this?* I thought. I'd have to take it easy on the girls, but I soon realized that the girls were actually much stronger than I was, and they twisted me up like the kid working at Wetzel's Pretzel. Once I was paired with a really attractive blond girl. It sounded awesome on paper, but it turned out to be my most embarrassing jujitsu experience yet. Before I could even think about flirting with her, she tucked my head under her shoulders and put me in the familiar guillotine choke. The rest of the class looked on as my face turned blue. I barely managed to tap out before I passed out. Then we'd start again and I'd get caught in another submission. Five minutes into this utter humiliation, things got even worse. I got a boner. This rare physical contact with the opposite sex was more action than I'd gotten in a year. Instead of looking like a pervert with a BDSM fetish, I immediately tapped out before she could notice my boner. I was TKO'd by my own dick. I rushed over and grabbed my gym bag to cover my boner and then sidestepped out of the gym. I never went back ever again.

The only female contact I'd gotten lately was getting my ass handed to me in jujitsu. I was destined to be unemployed and play *Madden* with Phil at my dad's for the rest of my life. And that's when I googled "local open mics." When people google "local open mics," they are one step away from googling "What's the least painful way to kill myself?" It's the last frontier before giving up on life.

My search results led me to the HaHa Cafe Comedy Club in North Hollywood. It was the only legitimate comedy club in LA that had an open mic every night at six before their real shows. The catch was I had to pay five dollars to get five minutes of stage time, only to perform in front of five other open-mic comics who were impatiently waiting their turn. Sounds terrible? It totally was. But as bad as it was, it was still better than wasting my life away. My life was so lame at that point that paying money to embarrass myself at an open mic was somehow an improvement. Almost every comedian I've met started doing stand-up after some kind of crisis in his or her life. Sometimes it's a bad divorce, a bankruptcy or a third DUI arrest. For me, it was getting a boner at jujitsu class. The next day, I drove to the Haha Comedy Club and paid my five dollars to get onstage for the very first time. I wasn't nervous at all. I mean, what did I have to lose? My dignity? That was left behind on the jujitsu mat.

So many of my favorite urban comedians and all of my favorite rappers went by stage names: Cedric the Entertainer, Bruce Bruce, Snoop Dogg, Jay-Z. I thought I needed my own catchy stage name. So I signed up on my first open mic as "Lowball Jim." I had seen that name in a Texas hold 'em instruction guide online, where there were two players facing off, Highball Phil and Lowball Jim. I thought it'd be funny to get introduced as a shady-sounding Lowball Jim and this little innocent-looking Asian kid would pop up.

"Our next comedian, Lowball Jim!"

I jumped up onstage and got my first chuckles.

"What's up, North Hollywood!" I learned that from BET *Comicview*: always start by shouting the city you're in. The crowd responded with a few mechanical claps, and by crowd I mean the five other comedians who were waiting their turn to get onstage.

I then rambled on with five minutes of masturbation jokes, the gold standard for all new comics who haven't learned the meaning of the word *hack*. And my closer was yet another masturbation bit:

"I was jerking off to porn on my computer and watching ESPN at the same time. And right when I was about to finish, Michael Vick scores a touchdown and I turned around to the TV and came. So basically, I jacked off to Michael Vick." With a few pity chuckles, the legend of Lowball Jim was born.

All the comedians hung out at the bar after the shows and talked about our sets. Everyone was giving each other tips for their bits; it reminded me of writing rhymes at Chris's house.

A fellow open-miker came up to me. "Yo, that Michael Vick bit was funny. Can I give you a tag?"

I didn't know what tag meant but, "Sure." Apparently, tags are additional funny lines tagged after the punch line.

"At the end of the bit you can say, 'So now every time Michael Vick scores a touchdown, I cum a little.'"

I laughed. This was brilliant. I didn't think anyone would care for the stupid Michael Vick jerk-off joke. But this guy was actually analyzing it and helping me improve on it. I felt like I was welcomed into a secret society of comedians. This new world where jerking off to Michael Vick was considered an art form was exactly what I was looking for.

Even though stand-up was a one-man sport, it was a community of hilarious people. There were comedians from every background: black, white, Asian, Latino, twenties, fifties, rich, poor, single, divorced, red-blooded Americans and immigrants. Comedy doesn't care about where you are from; it cares about how funny you are. Comedians are some of the most cynical and judgmental people, but we judge each other on the content of our jokes, not the color of our skin. Martin Luther King would be proud of the stand-up community. As long as you're funny, it doesn't matter if you're rich or poor, Nigerian or Chinese, skinny or fat. Funny is funny. Stand-up comedy is one of the only places where all the out-siders truly fit in. It is like a secret society for the disenfranchised. It's the only place where the weirder you are, the more interesting you become. Stand-up comedy was one of the only places I felt like I truly belonged.

THE GODFATHER

When I went back to San Diego to finish my shameful fifth year of college, I went to every comedy club in San Diego in hopes for some stage time, and everyone told me: "If you want to do stand-up in San Diego, you need to talk to Sean Kelly." *Who is this mysterious Sean Kelly character? Is he a comedy club owner? Is he Dave Chappelle's cousin?* Everyone seemed to know him, but nobody wanted to tell me where to find him. I needed to hunt him down if I wanted to be part of the San Diego comedy scene.

I went home and did some research on Sean Kelly. Through a Google search, I found that Sean was the owner of a public-speaker agency where you could hire anyone from Bill Clinton to Scottie Pippen. I was enamored by all the celebrities I saw on that website. At that point, the only celebrity I knew was Kevin Sorbo. Then I saw Sean was performing at the Comedy Palace in San Diego that weekend, so I went down there and stalked down this mystery man.

I told the doorman at the Comedy Palace I was a comedian, and he let me right in free of charge. That's the secret to any com-edy club; just say you're a comedian and they'll let you right in. And if you say you're "industry," meaning an agent or manager, the doorman might actually pay you to come in. Everyone in a comedy club wants to get signed. It's the training ground for desperate artists.

I finally got my first glimpse of Sean when the host introduced him. He was an unassuming middle-aged bald white guy who definitely wasn't Dave Chappelle's cousin. But he was funny as hell. I waited for him backstage like an excited fangirl at a Justin Bieber concert. Finally, he walked past me and I saw my chance to introduce myself.

"Hi, Sean. I saw you owned a public-speaker agency. How does that work?"

And just like a mob boss, Sean said, "Take a seat." My research paid off. He started dropping some serious knowledge on me. He told me:

"The speaker agency is a side thing I started. You can make money doing stand-up, but you can make a lot of money being a public speaker. We should all do both. Comedians don't think about that. We are already great public speakers."

Sean was a master businessman. I learned that the Comedy Palace was a Greek restaurant during the day called the Greek Palace. Business was slow at the Greek Palace, so Sean convinced its owner to let him run a comedy show there at night. Eventually, that turned into a full-fledged comedy club with its own staff. Sean told me, "Instead of begging for stage time at other comedy clubs, I started my own comedy club."

When other comics were talking about jerking off, Sean was talking about business plans. Whenever Sean talked, he captured your full, undivided attention. Some people can sell ice to an Eskimo; Sean can sell a Home Depot utility belt to Batman. And his ultimate gift was helping others discover their story.

"Where are you from?" Sean asked me.

"I went to high school in LA, but I was born in Hong Kong."

"How old were you when you came to LA?"

"I was thirteen. I couldn't really speak English yet, so I learned how to speak English by watching BET," I jokingly told him the truth.

Sean didn't laugh, but he took it all in. "That's what you need to talk about in your stand-up. You have a great story and you have a different point of view. Talk about that in your set. Then once you have all your stories written down, you can even write a book."

And here I am, writing that book. I'd never met anyone who had such a high-caliber creative motor within a clever business mind. I hung on to everything Sean said. He became my mentor and my comedy godfather.

Along with his many talents, Sean was also a licensed auctioneer. He did charity auctions, police impound auctions and storage unit auctions. He'd later use his skills to pitch the reality show *Storage Hunters*, where he played the auctioneer. To many in the US, *Storage Hunters* might be the lesser-known version of *Storage Wars,* but *Storage Hunters* eventually became one of the biggest reality shows in the UK.

Sean and his wife, Lori, would eventually move to the UK where strangers stopped him every two steps to take a selfie. Not only was he selling out shows as a comedian, he had made himself a celebrity in the UK. We've become family over the years. Lori once asked Sean, "Can we just adopt Jimmy?" And Sean said, "I'm pretty sure Jimmy has real parents. And he's way past his prime adoption age."

FIRST JOB IN SHOW BIZ

The Comedy Palace became my new hangout. It became my fraternity that I never had at UCSD. We had a hundred new people coming to watch our sets and we drank on the house every night. We even had a waitress that used to work as a stripper at Cheetahs. I mean what more can you ask for in a fraternity?

I was hanging out at the Comedy Palace so much, they eventually hired me as the doorman. I seated the audience members in exchange for ten minutes of stage time and two hours of minimum wage. It was always a challenge to seat the audience and then try to be a comedian onstage. Everyone in the audience was asking themselves, *Hey, isn't that the kid who just sat us? I guess they just let anybody do stand-up here.* I took on the challenge. It was so much sweeter when I made them laugh after they thought I was just a doorman. I got paid fifteen dollars a night as the doorman, but I got paid nothing for my sets as a comedian. I was just happy to get some legitimate stage time that wasn't an open mic.

One of my favorite comedians at the Palace was Tarrell Wright. Tarrell was a hilarious black dude from Detroit. His brother Kool-Aid was a famous urban comedian that used to be on BET *Comicview*. Needless to say, I looked up to him. Tarrell was so funny that nobody really wanted to follow him onstage, so he always went up last at the Comedy Palace shows. He was just as funny offstage as he was onstage. He'd always give me old-school player dating advice that his dad had passed on to him. "If you fuck her mind, you fuck her all the time." I didn't even know what that really meant, but it sounded cool as hell.

Then there was Guam Felix, who's literally from the US territory of Guam. Imagine if my name was Hong Kong Jim; that would actually sound way more gangster than Lowball Jim. Guam was a forty-year-old veteran comedian who was a former strip club DJ. His goal in life was winning the lottery. He'd preface everything with:

"When I win the lottery . . ." But he didn't even have ambitious goals for if he did win the lottery. He'd always tell me:

"When I win the lottery, dog, we are all going to HomeTown Buffet."

"Guam, you don't have to win a fifty-million-dollar lottery to go to the HomeTown Buffet, it's eleven ninety-nine."

"Yeah, but we can go there every day!"

Tarrell once said, "Guam is the ghettoest motherfucker I've ever known." That speaks volumes coming from a guy who grew up in the hood, in Detroit.

All of the comedians helped out in the club. Every week, we folded envelopes with promotional mailers in the back room of the Comedy Palace. I never minded the extra work; I got to hang out with some of the most hilarious people in the city. We were late on sending the promotional mailers one week and all the comedians stayed up to pull an all-nighter in the back of the Palace. Tarrell, Guam and I along with five other comedians were tediously folding envelopes like a bunch of Chinese sweatshop workers. It was four in the morning and we were trying our best to keep each other awake. Guam asked Tarrell:

"Hey, T, how many girls have you slept with?"

Tarrell tried to do some math in his head but quickly gave up. "Phew, I don't even know." Either he had amnesia or it was so many he simply lost count. I couldn't imagine a day where I would lose count of the women I'd slept with. At that time, I could count on one hand; honestly, I could have counted with one finger. Guam continued:

"I'd guess it's probably around the same number as me."
Tarrell: "Probably. How many for you?"
Without skipping a beat, Guam answered:
"One sixty. Half of them were strippers when I DJ'd at the strip club."

Holy shit, is that even a possible number? I'd never even talked to a hundred and sixty women, and definitely not eighty strippers! My mind couldn't comprehend such an astronomical number. What was even more surprising was that this seemed completely normal to everyone else. Nobody flinched or asked any further questions. They just nodded in agreement. Tarrell calmly acquiesced: "Yeah, that sounds about right." So I kept my mouth shut and acted like everything was normal, while my brain melted with shock and envy.

Guam then turned to Robert, a shyish comedian on the other side of the table. "Yo, Robert, what about you?" *Okay, maybe Guam and Tarrell are just crazy. I'm glad to hear a normal guy like Robert's perspective.* Given that he was forty and fairly handsome, I was guessing eight.

"Man, I lost count after, like, sixty."
What the fuck?! Robert too?!
Guam casually pressed on: "It's gotta be over three digits though, right?"
"Yeah, I think around there, I don't know. One time a girl came up to me and said, 'Hey, remember me?' And I had no idea who she was. Apparently I had sex with her before."
Did everyone have sex with a hundred women but me?

Everyone laughed as Guam reached across the table to give Robert a high-five. I sat there, shell-shocked. For me, the thought of having sex with a hundred women was like thinking about the vastness of the universe; it's unfathomable for a meager human brain. And just then, Guam pivoted to me.

"Jimmy, what about you?"

I looked up at him in a confused panic, like the soldier who was holding his own severed arm in *Saving Private Ryan*.

"Me?" I stalled. "Ummm, like . . ."

I pretended to count in my head.

Guam started laughing. "What? Like six?"

Everyone cracked up.

Six is six times more than my real number. And they are laughing at that?

I broke out in a cold sweat. My number was so off, I didn't even know how to lie. I just nodded and agreed. "Yeah, something like that."

"Yo, we gotta get Jimmy laid!" Guam screamed out.

"Shit, Jimmy don't even know what pussy is yet," Tarrell added.

That night I felt like I needed to crawl under my bed and re-evaluate my entire life and have a real heart-to-heart with my penis. I wanted to be cool like Guam. Even though he was dreaming to win the lottery, I looked up to his sexual prowess. Hong Kong Jim wanted to DJ in a strip club just like Guam Felix.

Stand-up comedy was my first experience with the real world after being institutionalized in school my entire life. What's normal in the stand-up comedy world was far from normal in the real world. Going to sleep at three in the morning, waking up at

The boys from the Comedy Palace. Tarrell Wright (left), Guam Felix (right) and Lowball Jim. I looked like an aspiring scumbag.

noon and dreaming of becoming a strip club DJ. Even though I knew something was off about this world, I wanted to fit in with my frat brothers. The Comedy Palace was my only escape from my lousy real life, and I was loving every moment in this alternate universe. I'd show up during the day to take reservations on the phone, seat the audience in the evening and then fold envelopes at night. If they had let me sleep there, I'd have fully moved into the Comedy Palace. I even brought my Xbox to the back room. I'd call Tarrell during the afternoon, five hours before the show.

"Yo, Tarrell, wanna come get your ass kicked in *NBA 2K*?"

"I'll see you at the club, bitch."

Reality always strikes when you're having too much fun. I was finally finding some meaning to my life at the Comedy Palace, but I soon realized my sixty-dollar weekly paycheck wasn't paying the bills. I was living way below the poverty line, even for a comedian. I ate instant ramen with a ninety-nine-cent can of Vienna sausages five nights out of the week. I'd save up enough money to go to either Denny's or pig out at HomeTown Buffet once a month. Maybe Guam was right about trying to win the lottery. I was praying for a car to plow into me so I could get some insurance settlement. My dad was right all along: "Pursuing your dreams is for losers. Doing what you love is how you become homeless."

I approached one of the managers at the Comedy Palace about my dire financial situation, hoping he'd give me a raise from seven fifty to eight dollars an hour. "Jimmy, you're great, but there are plenty of desperate comedians out there who would kill for minimum wage," he frankly explained to me. And he was right. I had zero leverage on asking for a fifty-cent raise. He advised, "Why don't you ask around for a second job? All the comedians here have day jobs." "I don't know, I don't think anybody wants to hire me," my low self-esteem responded. "Dude, everyone loves you here, just ask the next person who comes in the door." And just like a trite sitcom plot, the door swung open and Jay, a middle-aged comedian, entered. I turned to him.

"Jay, where do you work?"
"I sell used cars."
"Can I get a job with you?"
"Yeah, sure, come down to the lot, I'll get you a job."

And that's how I became a comedian/used-car salesman. Apparently, you need zero qualifications to become a used-car salesman, just like becoming a stand-up comedian.

The dealership was a crummy used-car lot that specialized in selling shitty old cars to people with bad credit. Our customers' credit scores were so bad, when no other car lot in the city would sell them a tricycle, we'd jump in to sell them a 1998 Dodge Neon at a 24 percent interest rate. It doesn't take a master salesman when you're people's last resort. Our slogan was "Either you buy our shitty car or you can take the bus."

The car lot manager, Larry, was a sixty-year-old veteran car salesman and a career alcoholic. He would vanish from the lot for days at a time to go on a binge. Then he would make a miraculous comeback from the dead and push ten Dodge Neons in a week. I never judged Larry based on his addiction, and I looked up to him as a top-notch car pusher. I learned a lot of old-school salesmanship from Larry and soon became the young hotshot at the shittiest used-car lot in town. It might not have been Smith Barney, but I felt like a baller who could afford HomeTown Buffet once a week. I knew if I worked hard, someday, just maybe, I'd be able to afford Red Lobster.

HOW TO HANDLE RACIST HECKLERS

Getting onstage was a tremendous high and I was hooked. For the fleeting moment when i was onstage, I was able to forget about all my life's problems and be truly in the moment. I've seen comedians trade money, weed and sexual favors for stage time. If stand-up is your addiction, stage time is your crack. During my first two years of stand-up, I did seven to ten sets a week and I didn't get paid for a single one of those early sets. I would do any type of show, at any venue, in any situation. I've done stand-up at a nursing home before bingo night and I've performed at a children's party where I had to compete with Spider-Man for their attention. My friend who ran a bar in San Diego asked me to do his Monday stand-up show at his bar. "It's a fun show, the crowd's a little rowdy, but it's a good crowd. You should come do it." I needed a hit of that crack.

It was a particularly seedy dive bar in the south side of San Diego. All the patrons drove lifted pickup trucks, wore cargo shorts and drank Bud Light. When he told me the crowd was "a little rowdy," what he actually meant was the crowd was a bunch of drunk racist assholes. I don't like to toss around the word *racist* lightly, but in this instance it was quite justified. Before I went onstage that night, someone in the crowd booed another comedian and the rest of the crowd cheered. Then another drunk dude in the audience heckled, "You suck!" The comedian was flustered. Then another heckler randomly screamed out, "Nigger!" The heckle made no sense; the comedian was white. This piece of human trash just thought it was funny to scream out a nasty racial slur. What's even worse was that the crowd loved it; they cheered in agreement. I thought to myself, *Well, tonight is the night I die.* I badly wanted that stage time, though. I was willing to dangle my little Asian body in front of a bunch of racist fools who looked like gator wranglers from the show *Swamp People.* I knew I had to do something different than my normal material to survive that night. So I decided to take a chance. Right before it was my turn to go onstage, I went over to the DJ, who was just some local drunk with an iPod, and I asked him to play a particular song when I got onstage. When the host brought me up—"Okay, give it up for our next comedian!"—the song came on:

"Everybody was kung-fu fighting! Those kicks were fast as lightning!"
The crowd busted out in laughter.
I jumped onto the stage and screamed into the microphone:
"What's up, you racist motherfuckers!"

I was either going to win them over or get stabbed in the back of my neck. I might have pissed myself a little bit, but I didn't let it show on my face. Then the whole place erupted into laughter. I got them by the balls and they paid attention to the rest of my set like a bunch of studious honor students. I doubled down on material about being Chinese. They loved it.

"I can't go to Chinese restaurants with white people any-more," I proclaimed in front of a room full of the whitest people. "Every time I go to a Chinese restaurant, my white friends always ask me, 'Jimmy, you speak Mandarin? Bro, order in Mandarin, it's going to be hilarious! They are going to hook us up!'" I stared at my imaginary white friend. "Bro, we are in Panda Express. Her name tag says Conseula."

The crowd ate it up like it was orange chicken with a side of chow mein. I went on to have one of my best sets yet. I didn't get paid a single penny that night, but I did score a six-pack of Bud Light. There were no rules in stand-up. It was the opposite of college; it was all the creative freedom I had ever wanted. I lived and breathed stand-up, and all I could think about was how to improve my bits. It made me forget I was a total disappointment to my dad. This was the burning passion that Mike Judge described in his commencement speech when he found animation. It was clear that I had finally found my calling in stand-up comedy.

TOP FIVE NONMONETARY PAYMENTS FOR A STAND-UP SET

1. Weed
2. High-fives
3. Unsolicited career advice
4. One food item from the left side of the menu
5. A used copy of *FIFA 2013*

I GOT *ARSENIO* CANCELED

Six years later, I made my stand-up debut on TV on the revival of *The Arsenio Hall Show*. Growing up on urban culture, performing in front of the Dog Pound on *Arsenio* was my equivalent of performing on Johnny Carson's *The Tonight Show*. The guest performances were usually booked months in advance, but I got an urgent call from their booker on a Wednesday. "A comedian dropped out of Friday's show, do you want to do it?" Abso-fucking-lutely. I had two days to prepare, and no time to overthink it.

I wanted to look fresh for my debut, so I went to Nordstrom with a five-hundred-dollar limit on my credit card. The show was going to send a limo to pick me up; I couldn't just hop in with my Ross basketball shorts. I'd never bought anything at a Nordstrom before; I could barely afford Nordstrom Rack. I bought a two-hundred-dollar pair of jeans and a nice polo shirt at full retail price. My mother would have had a heart attack. "Jimmy! You spent two hundred dollars on those jeans?! Are you crazy?! I can buy you five pairs in China for ten dollars!" The old-country guilt still ran deep in my DNA, but I wanted to feel like an American baller for once in my life.

When the limo picked me up from my crummy apartment that Friday afternoon, my confused neighbors probably thought I was going to high school prom. I arrived at the studio and was ushered into my very own greenroom. I realized how far I'd come from folding envelopes in the back room of the Comedy Palace. The show had just started and I was scheduled to be the closing performance. Arsenio was doing his thing, riling up the Dog Pound with his opening monologue. His first guest was Tom Bergeron, the host of *Dancing with the Stars* and *America's Funniest Home Videos*, who I grew up watching with my family back in Hong Kong. It was surreal to be watching the show on a TV backstage, knowing that I'd be teleported onto that television set in just a few minutes. I was a nervous wreck. I chugged as many free Fiji water bottles as I could in the greenroom, to make up for my two-hundred-dollar jeans. A production assistant knocked on the door. "You're on in five minutes." I took a much-needed pee and I walked backstage. It was surreal when Arsenio introduced me to the Dog Pound. "Give it up, for Jimmy O. Yang, ladies and gentlemen!" *Wow, Arsenio Hall, the "urban" Johnny Carson, now knows my name.* I walked out to an uproarious audience in the Dog Pound, and I was ready. All those hours studying BET *Comicview* were finally going to pay off; this was my *Comicview* moment.

I rolled off my set with my trusted self-deprecating opener: "I can't take my shirt off at the beach. I'm in shape, but I'm just a small guy with really nice hair. So from the back I look like a hot Asian chick. And from the front . . . I look like a really hot Asian chick."

The crowd applauded. I got them.

Then I went on with the bit about how I learned English from BET *Rap City,* the bit Sean Kelly encouraged me to write. The Dog Pound loved it. I felt confident, and pointed over to Arsenio and said, "Me and Arsenio, we are going to do *Rush Hour 4."* Even Arsenio was clapping on the other side of the stage. I rolled on with the rest of my routine and stuck the landing with my Maury bit, where I observed that I'd never seen an Asian guy on the Maury Povich show, followed by an act-out of a fresh-off-the boat Asian guy on Maury. "Look, Maury, look. He has big eye and I have small eye. That's not my baby, Maury!" To my absolute surprise, the audience stood up and gave me a standing ovation. All the time watching BET, all the time I spent at the Comedy Palace and all the crappy unpaid gigs I'd done had culminated in this moment on national television. "Give it up for him!" Arsenio hollered at the audience. He even did a callback on my joke. "Also check my website because *Rush Hour 4* is coming, y'all!" He gave me a hug and whispered:

"You did it. You did it."

Those three words meant everything to me. They validated my questionable decision to quit Smith Barney and pursue stand-up comedy. They validated the past six years spent at comedy clubs and dive bars. It was the first time someone had ever told me, "You did it." I felt like I finally did something right with my life. I looked up at the audience one last time; tears welled up in my eyes.

Backstage, Arsenio joked, "This is gonna be the last time you ever talk to me, you'll be too famous to talk to me after this."

"Thank you so much for having me on your show, Arsenio. I'm sure I'll talk to you again, hopefully I'll be on this show again."

"You got it, man, would love to have you back."

I never got to go back on the show again. Three days later, *The Arsenio Hall Show* was abruptly canceled. CBS had originally signed on for a second season before I went on the show, but they decided to pull the plug on it three days after I went on. Coincidence? Probably. Or maybe this hot Asian chick was too hot for America. Either way, I felt lucky that someone dropped out so I became the very last stand-up comedian to ever perform on *The Arsenio Hall Show*, joining the likes of Eddie Murphy, George Lopez and Andrew "Dice" Clay. On my following birthday, Jeremy gave me a custom-made poster that said: YOU GOT ARSENIO CANCELED. I now proudly hang this magnificent poster in my living room, as I will cherish this moment forever.

Rush Hour 4?

CHAPTER SIX

HOW TO STRIP CLUB DJ

The names of the people in this chapter have been changed in order to protect their identities and my safety. Yes, this chapter is about to get gangster.

I'd only been to a strip club once in my life when I was eighteen years old. Phil took me to a high-end strip club with velvet curtains and chandeliers in Westwood in LA. I was blown away by how beautiful the dancers were. They didn't look like strippers; they looked like sorority girls from USC. They probably were actual USC students trying to pay off the astronomical tuition. I was not a very confident eighteen-year-old, and I was sure the strippers could smell the virgin on me. Phil offered to buy me a lap dance but I was afraid of the unknown behind those VIP curtains, so I turned it down. I wasn't interested in throwing money behind the brass railing in exchange for a pair of blue balls. I wanted to be an insider who knew these girls on a real-name basis. I wanted to be a strip club DJ just like Guam. Guam was definitely no role model, but my young and impressionable libido was incredibly envious of him sleeping with eighty strippers. Becoming a strip club DJ was the only way to instantly transform myself from a sexually frustrated chump to a world-class stripper whisperer. Being a strip club DJ became my American dream.

I was working at the used car lot during the day and then putting in work at the Comedy Palace every night. Old Larry at the car lot had a friend named Shooter who came to visit him at the lot every week. They knew each other from AA or 'Nam or something, I forget. I think it was AA. Or maybe it was AA in 'Nam. Larry lived in Shooter's apartment. When you are sixty years old and you still crash at a buddy's apartment, you know you have made some serious mistakes in your life. Shooter was a notorious figure in the San Diego underworld. Word on the streets, Shooter did twenty years of hard time in prison for something involving a dead body. I didn't dare to dig any deeper. He wasn't affiliated with any particular gangs, but all the gangs respected him. Shooter also owned a strip club in San Diego.

Shooter was in his sixties; he rocked a thin Mohawk and wore a pair of black plastic Choppers sunglasses. Have you ever looked at a guy and you know he could kill you without flinching? Well, Shooter looked like he would beat that guy to death with a sledgehammer. Whenever he entered a room, he exuded a dark aura of power. He was like the Undertaker from the WWE, except this was real-life hellfire and brimstone. I was scared, but absolutely fascinated by him. Every time Shooter came in, I looked up at him in awe. I thought gangsters were so cool, let alone a gangster who owned a strip club. Larry had told Shooter that I did stand-up and Shooter quickly took an interest in my comedy. He probably noticed the admiration in my eyes. The first time he talked to me, I was as nervous as a nerdy high school freshman talking to the starting varsity quarterback.

"Hey, kid, I heard you do stand-up," Shooter said to me in his gravelly Mickey Rourke voice.

Even though I knew he was a gangster, I tried to stay composed and talk to him like any normal person. "Yeah, I'm usually at the Comedy Palace. You should come by sometime," I replied.

"Sounds good. I can bring some of the girls from the club." In case you're wondering, by "girls" he meant strippers. I could barely contain my excitement. I couldn't wait to show off my soon-to-be stripper fans to the boys at the Comedy Palace.

I realized talking to gangsters is like talking to celebrities; you just have to treat them like normal people and not freak out over who they are. They don't like to be treated differently; they just want a genuine conversation like everyone else. Gangsters have feelings too.

That weekend, Shooter rolled up to the Comedy Palace in a white stretch limo. One by one the ~~strippers~~ girls strutted out of his car. Everyone in the parking lot stopped and stared. I proudly whispered to Guam and Tarrell, "That's my boy, Shooter." Guam nodded in approval. And without taking his eyes off the girls, all Tarrell said was, "Damn!" It was one of the coolest moments of my life.

That night, I felt like a gangster myself. When you are on the good side of a gangster, you feel safe and invincible. All the comedians were extra motivated that night and we put on a killer show. I could see Shooter and the girls clapping their hands, laughing like innocent children. For a moment, Shooter went from a feared gangster to a regular, happy audience member. That's the magical thing about stand-up comedy. No matter who the audience member might be, if you can make him laugh, you've got a fan for life.

After the show, the girls came up to me one after another to give me a hug. "Oh my God, you were so funny!" "Hilarious!" "That was amazing!" These positive affirmations from the strippers felt as legit as a raving *New York Times* review. Sean, Tarrell, Guam and all the other comedians looked on in awe. I got all the street cred I could ever wish for that night.

Then Shooter walked over to me and simply said, "Good job" as he made his way into his limo. I knew this was my chance; I saw my American dream of working at a strip club flash in front of my eyes. I seized the moment and I ducked my head in the limo before Shooter closed the door.

"Hey, do you need a new DJ for your club?" I nervously blurted out.

"You free this Thursday?"

FUCK. YES.

FANTASY SHOWGIRLS

I couldn't sleep for the next few days. I felt like a kid who just got the golden ticket to Shooter's Stripper Factory. All the years of sexual frustration in high school and college would finally be forgotten. This would be my ultimate redemption from Guam and Tarrell making fun of me in the back of the Comedy Palace. I pictured the hottest strippers surrounding me as I spun on the ones and twos at a fancy strip club that was like a kind of heaven for dudes.

When I stepped foot into Shooter's club on Thursday, I realized it was nothing like the paradise I had imagined. It was inside an old wooden bungalow in the shady part of town. The exterior was pink and powder blue with an old wooden sign that read: FANTASY SHOWGIRLS. There were no velvet curtains or chandeliers. I entered through a giant wooden door and swam through some old crusty purple curtains, and there I was, in the shittiest strip club I had ever seen. It was nothing like the swanky strip club Phil had taken me to in Westwood. If the Westwood strip club was a Michelin-star restaurant, this strip club would be a taco truck on the side of a gas station. It was a seedy, dystopian joint where dreams came to die. The inside smelled like years of despair and ball sweat, with a hint of stripper lotion. To this day, I'm not sure what strippers put on their bodies, but every stripper wears that same distinct stripper lotion. Nowadays, that smell brings me a satisfying nostalgia. The chairs and VIP booths were old Goodwill-quality pieces with suspicious stains on them, but the lights were just dark enough that you could trick your mind into not seeing them. There was a bar in the middle of the club. It was a sad, lonely island that only served sodas and Red Bulls. Under California state law, a fully nude club cannot serve any alcoholic beverages; only a topless club can serve alcohol, and ours was the fully nude variety. I never really understood that law. I guess the lawmakers thought the exposure of vaginas mixed with alcohol was the tipping point that would make people's brains explode or something. Everyone knew this; customers just showed up wasted anyways. It was a sound strategy for veteran perverts.

The DJ booth sat a few steps aboveground. It was a five-foot-square dim wooden box, featuring a simple sawed-out view hole. It had a good vantage point of the whole place, like the sniper towers in San Quentin. The booth had an old Dell computer with all the favorite strip club music, from Mötley Crüe to Jeremih. Other than the sound system and microphone, the most essential part of a strip club DJ booth is the light board. Lighting in a strip club is just as important as the music. Different girls look better in different lights. For instance, I learned that black girls always look better in green light. Not trying to start some new racial stereotype. It's just a fact. Try it sometime.

A tall, intimidating man greeted me. "You're the new DJ? I'm Beast." He was the bouncer who, in fact, looked like a beast. Beast was probably in his thirties, but a lifetime of meth and alcohol made him look like a weathered fifty-year-old. He was a skinny six-foot-four white guy with a cleanly shaven head and tattoos on his face. I later learned that he was a member of the Aryan Brotherhood when he was in prison, so I'm sure he wasn't too hot on this little Chinese boy spinning at his club. Beast claimed to be a recovering alcoholic, but I'd always see him in the bathroom with a plastic Smirnoff bottle at the end of his shift. I never had any problems with him, but we never really had a heart-to-heart over a nice bottle of wine, either. He always kept to his Aryan self.

Everyone at the club had nicknames, the kind you earn in prison. A man named Chef was the bar manager. He was short, but tough. Chef looked like if Joe Pesci was on welfare. As a bartender he was responsible for overcharging the customers for a splash of Mountain Dew, but more importantly, he was responsible for keeping everyone in check. Chef was in charge of making sure everything was operating smoothly at the club. He was Shooter's trusted old-school boy. One time, Chef told me:

> "I was out of action for a year. Now I'm trying to get back on the grind."
> I naively asked, "Why were you out for a year?"
> "I lost my big toe."

It doesn't get more gangster than losing your big toe. I was guessing he lost it because he owed some money to some bad people. This is the kind of stuff you only hear about in Martin Scorsese movies.

> "How did you lose it?" I sheepishly asked.
> "Diabetes."
> Diabetes doesn't care if you're a gangster, it'll fuck you up.

I was never intimidated by Beast and Chef. I thought they were super cool real-life gangsters, but I always treated them like normal coworkers. After getting to know them, I soon realized none of them really wanted to be where they were in life; they just fell into it because of a tough upbringing, drugs or alcohol. If they had a choice to put on a tie and work an honest living at a bank, they would. But the mistakes they made in the past haunted them and would always follow them around. It wasn't "cool" for them to work at a strip club; it was the absolute last resort. And the same could be said about the strippers.

We had an eclectic group of strippers at Fantasy Showgirls. It was like a brochure for community college dropouts. We had an Asian girl fittingly named Jade; a Latina girl uninspiringly named Latina; and two black girls named Milan and Saucy, although every week Milan would change her name to a different city she had never been to. I always thought that was ambitious of her. Saucy was indeed very saucy. She would talk trash and start physical fights with the other strippers. These were definitely not USC students working their way through college; these were career strippers who looked like strippers.

I once came into work to witness Milan and Saucy wrestling on the ground. Beast and Chef just casually stood there, passively saying, "Hey, guys, break it up." Breaking up a stripper fight is very similar to dealing with little kids throwing a tantrum. The more you yell at them, the more they are going to yell back. All you can really do is to stay calm and wait for them to tucker themselves out. The stripper fights didn't involve a lot of punches. They went directly for the most expensive part on a stripper; the weave. A winner was determined when one stripper successfully removed the other's weave. Saucy got the better of Milan that night. Milan put up a good fight but I think she just rocked a loose weave. That was the first time I saw a weave detached from a girl's head. I was caught off guard. They never taught me the anatomy of a stripper's weave in health class. Underneath the weave, Milan looked like a fry cook with a netted cap.

One of my jobs was to make sure the strippers went onstage in a timely manner. I always ruled by kindness. I was not trying to be a saint; this was merely a work strategy. I was trying to bring professionalism into a shitty strip club. I wanted to give these strippers something they had never experienced before: a man who was genuinely kind to them. On the business end, this worked brilliantly. Their shifts were always on time. The girls rotated every three songs like a group of Olympic synchronized strippers. But it didn't help me in scoring with any of the girls. I guess nice guys do always finish last, especially in a strip club. As a nice strip club DJ, I became a trusted friend of the strippers. This also meant I became the last guy they wanted to have sex with. They would sit next to me naked and talk to me about their boyfriends, and I would sit there and nod my head, trying to conceal my boner.

I didn't even think being friend-zoned by strippers was possible, but I made it happen. I watched naked women dance in front of me every day, but I still couldn't get laid. The strippers sat in the DJ booth naked and told me about their problems, but I still couldn't get laid. There was a stripper giving a hand job ten feet away from me in a VIP booth, but I. Still. Couldn't. Get. Laid. I couldn't imagine a more sexually frustrating experience. I had such blue balls my scrotum looked like the Cookie Monster. I wanted to be Guam Felix, but I was just the good innocent Hong Kong Jim. I was actually innocent enough to have a crush on one of the strippers.

Paige was a beautiful nineteen-year-old girl who was our new-est dancer. I had a crush on her the moment she walked into the club in her Daisy Dukes. Paige looked like a bright college girl who didn't belong in a strip club. She always had the cutest smile on her face. The main reason I wanted to work in a strip club was to hook up with a couple of strippers, but Paige—I would marry Paige. She was the girl next door from a Nicholas Sparks movie. I was head over heels for this girl. After her three-song routine, she would always come by the DJ booth to have a chat. That was the highlight of my day. "How did I look out there?" she would ask me, with the prettiest smile on her face.

"You looked great." Trying to remain composed and not pro-pose to her in the strip club.

Then she would lean over me with her naked body and pick out the songs she liked for her next dance. "That new Jeremih song goes well with you," I suggested. I was pairing R&B songs with strippers like a sommelier at Spago suggesting which red goes best with the beef Bolognese.

This sounded like a romantic dialogue from a *Pretty Woman* sequel. I thought we were going to live happily ever after. But in reality, I was just an innocent schmuck and she was just doing her job. *Pretty Woman* is bullshit.

I walked her to her car every night, but I was always too shy to ask her for her number. Weeks went by and I still couldn't muster up the courage to ask her out. I finally gave myself an ultimatum. As I nervously walked her back to her car, I asked her, "You got any plans tonight?"

"I'm going to my boyfriend's house," she casually replied. My heart sank.

My crush had a boyfriend; that's a familiar scenario that I'd experienced consistently since middle school. My mind was in denial; it tried to keep my hopes alive, hoping maybe one day she would break up with him and run into my arms. Days went by and I was completely out of sorts. I had to talk to someone about this, so I talked to Shooter. Like a college roommate, I went up to Shooter and said, "Paige is pretty cool, huh?" Hoping to prompt him into a nice conversation about Paige.

Without skipping a beat, Shooter said, "Paige, she's a pathological liar, you shouldn't believe a word that comes out of her mouth."

Shocked and unconvinced, I asked, "Really? How do you know that?"

Shooter laughed and replied, "I fucked her."

My innocence died with those words.

LAP DANCE SALESMAN

Shooter taught me the most important thing about selling lap dances was the showcase. A showcase is when the DJ calls all the girls onto the stage for a roll call and pressures the customers to get lap dances. The designated song in our club was the classic strip club anthem "Girls, Girls, Girls" by Mötley Crüe. Shooter didn't have many rules, but he was very clear that that song must accompany every showcase. After every third stripper, I would play that song and belch out in my strip club DJ voice: "All right, gentlemen, it's time for our showcase! I want all my girls to the stage right now! We have Jade, Milan, Paige, and the oh-sooooo-sexy Sauceyyyyy. We are doing two-for-one lap dances right now! Get two lap dances with your favorite girl or get one lap dance with two of your favorite girls at the same time! Don't be shy and don't be tight with your wallet. I want everybody in the VIP! Two-for-one lap dances, next ten minutes, two-for-one lap dances right now!" I would keep repeating that until every customer got a lap dance. The club was never that busy, which meant I just kept screaming at two customers until they finally caved in to the pressure.

Combining the microphone skills I learned from being a comedian and my salesmanship from being a used car salesman, I became an incredible lap dance salesman. According to Shooter, lap dance sales went up 44 percent the first week I started working there. I never took Shooter as an accounting wiz, but apparently he was meticulously keeping record of every lap dance sold at his club like Ernst & Young. Shooter was very impressed. He told me I reminded him a lot of himself. It's always a good move to compliment someone, then tell him he reminds you of you; it's like patting yourself on the back using the other person's hand. Shooter started giving me more responsibilities at his establishment and really took me under his wing. I felt like Henry Hill earning the trust of Jimmy Conway in *Goodfellas*; I felt like a made guy.

Shooter trusted me so much, he started to have me deliver the cash box from the strip club to his house. In hindsight, this was such a stupidly dangerous job for someone without any protection. I could have easily gotten robbed or killed during my cash delivery trips. But at the time, I didn't put much thought into it;

I was just happy that Shooter entrusted me with his cash. Every night Chef would hand me the cash box and I would hop into my Toyota Celica and drive to Shooter's apartment at three in the morning.

At Shooter's apartment, there were always a couple of goons passed out on the couch. Till today, I'm not sure if they passed out because they had partied too hard, done too much drugs or that was just their permanent dwelling. I learned to not ask too many questions in a gangster environment. I was always on high alert. I knew there were guns, drugs and a lot of cash in that house. It was a volatile place. But then I'd see old Larry from the car lot there, and that eased my mind. It was like going to a new friend's house and seeing an old friend already chilling there playing video games, except Larry was usually binge-drinking instead of playing *Halo*.

One night, I struggled through the shift with a fever. I popped a couple Advils but it wasn't helping much. I made my usual 3:00 A.M. delivery to Shooter's house. There was a different vibe about Shooter that night; he was quiet and serious. I would usually just drop off the cash and leave, but Shooter wanted to have a talk with me. I was in no condition to have a serious talk with a gangster; I was ready to collapse from my illness. I told him I had a fever and I should probably go home, but he insisted I sit down in his kitchen.

He grabbed me a glass of water and said, "Take this." He put an unmarked bottle of pills in front of me.

I asked, "What's this?"

He simply replied, "It'll make you feel better." All I could hear was Denzel from *Training Day* saying, "Didn't know you like to get wet" after he tricked Ethan Hawke into smoking PCP, or as he put it, "Sherms. Dust. PCP. Primos. P-Dog."

I politely declined the pills and Shooter said, "It's not going to kill you. You don't trust me?" There was an intense moment of silence as I sat there, half coherent, contemplating my next moves. Should I just take the pill and hope for the best, or scamper out of the house and go into witness protection?

Shooter let out a rare laugh and said, "I was just kidding! It's just Vicodin, take some if you want." I took a deep breath, I might have peed my pants a little. Shooter's tone got serious again.

"You been doing a great job at the club, kid, and everyone trusts you. I just came into some money and I'm going to be opening up a new club. I want you to run it for me."

Time stopped and my brain cranked into hyperfocus. I knew this was one of those life-changing crossroads. People always say your life comes down to a few key decisions that define you; this was clearly one of them. I had to decide if I wanted to become the underworld strip club king or continue to tell jokes at the Comedy Palace. For a twenty-two-year-old who watched too much BET *Rap City*, this was the toughest decision of my life. "Think about it," Shooter said. I spent the next three weeks thinking about nothing but that. It took spending Christmas at the strip club for me to finally decide on my path.

A STRIP CLUB CHRISTMAS

It was the saddest Christmas ever. I had no family in San Diego, so I went to my usual nine o'clock shift at the strip club on Christmas night. A few girls came in, hoping to make some money off people's sorrows. But the place was empty all night. I was actually pretty glad that it was; I would have felt really bad for whoever left their family behind to spend Christmas at a strip club. Chef called for an early midnight close. And just when we were about to shut our doors, a pair of drunken college kids around my age stumbled in. A tall white boy and his smaller Indian buddy; both were drunk as hell. Beast kindly told them to leave as we were already closed for the night, but these kids wouldn't take no for an answer. "It says on your Yelp page you close at two!" the tall one exclaimed. I was surprised we had a Yelp page too. Beast probably had no idea what Yelp was; I doubt he had to use it in prison. Beast calmly repeated, "We are closed for tonight." Still not satisfied, the smaller kid said, "That's bullshit!" Beast just stared at them with his murderous eyes. The pair finally thought better of it and stomped out. I was sure these kids were going to leave us a one-star review on Yelp, but we could care less. Our customers were not Yelpers.

I didn't think much of it and continued my closing routine, cleaning out my DJ booth and shutting down the old computer. Suddenly, Beast walked over to Chef and said, "They are still outside talking shit. Let's go." Without hesitation, Chef grabbed a two-by-four antique table leg that he had stashed behind the bar. "Motherfuckers," he said. He said it in such a determined way, I heard it like a war cry from Mel Gibson in *Braveheart*.

Chef and Beast romped out the door. I wasn't sure what to do, so I sheepishly followed a few steps behind. By the time I got outside, there was already a brawl in the middle of the street. Chef was beating the Indian kid with his antique table leg and the tall kid wrestled with Beast. I wanted to jump in, but I froze. My brain was smart enough to see what was going on and it stopped me from proceeding. I just stood there and watched it like a movie.

Chef swung his table leg and gave a couple good licks to the Indian kid's midsection. Then he rushed over to Beast, pulled the tall kid away from him and threw him to the ground. Beast gave him a hard kick to the midsection. The tall kid writhed in pain. The smaller guy got up slowly and started to limp off. Chef hit him with another stiff table leg to his ribs. The kid gasped, but barely any sound came out. There was a fear of death in their eyes as Chef stared them down. Chef and Beast finally relented before this turned into a homicide and the college kids hobbled away as fast as they could. Chef screamed out to the distance, "Don't walk, motherfucker! Run!" I stood there and I couldn't move. *Holy shit, what the fuck just happened?*

I was numb from fear, the fear of fighting, fear of getting arrested and fear for my own life. These were just a couple college kids like myself, but now I'm on the other side of this world. At that moment, I realized I'd joined the dark side. I was no longer a stupid college student like them; I was now on the other side as a grimy strip club employee who hung around gangsters. I finally had a sobering moment when I thought to myself, *Is this who I want to be? Do I really want to be a gangster?*

The next day, I tried to play it off like it was a cool story. I bragged to all my buddies at the Comedy Palace about what happened.

I told Tarrell, "I went outside with Chef and Beast, and those kids were scared. Chef beat the shit out of them with a table leg!

Then he screamed, 'Don't walk, motherfucker, run!' It was the most gangster shit ever."

I made myself sound like such a cool gangster dude. But deep down, I knew what happened was fucked up. Telling my friends was probably my therapy to cope with it. I felt completely out of control.

Then I received a call from Sean Kelly the next day. It was a bit odd for him to call me out of the blue during the day. Usually, we would just chat in person whenever I ran into him at the Comedy Palace. There was a sense of urgency to this call. I picked up the phone, and before I could say hi, Sean said:

"You need to get out of that strip club."

It was those words that gave me the ultimatum I needed. He had overheard the strip club Christmas brawl story from Tarrell, and he was very concerned. Sean said, "Jimmy, you are young, you are funny, move to LA and focus on your comedy. You need to get out of that strip club before it's too late." That was the wake-up call I so desperately needed.

I went to work at the strip club that night, but I knew it would be my last; it had to be. It was a quiet night. I was off my game. I wasn't playing the right songs and I was messing up stripper names. I called Milan "Paris," and she was not happy about that.

I was on edge all night, waiting for Shooter to come in for his nightly checkup. Shooter finally came in around midnight. For some reason he looked more intimidating than usual, or at least that's how I felt. I waited until he had greeted all the strippers and

I went up to him and said, "Shooter, I'm moving up to LA. I am quitting the strip club."

He didn't flinch. In a very matter-of-fact way, he said, "I was going to open up a new club for you and let you run it. You should stay."

Although flattered, I knew I had to stand my ground. I said, "I have to go to LA to pursue my comedy career."

As much as he wanted me to stay, he knew comedy was my passion and he respected that. So he simply said, "Okay" and he walked away. He understood. As much as Shooter wanted me to be his protégé, he knew I was destined for something bigger than his strip club. He let me go.

That was the last time I ever stepped foot into Fantasy Show-girls, or any strip club for that matter. After I moved to LA, Shooter kept in touch with me with a monthly phone call from a different number. I always had a feeling it was Shooter when I got a call from a random number with a 619 area code.

"Hello?"

"Hey, kid, everything good?" He never introduced himself, but I always recognized his voice.

"Hey, Shooter! Yeah, everything is great."

"Okay, just want to make sure you are all right," and he hung up. That was all he said, every time. He just wanted to know if I was okay, and nobody was fucking with me. It felt good to know a gangster had my back. I knew if anything were to happen to me, Shooter would take care of it. Shooter might have been a hard-nosed criminal, but he treated me like his son.

The calls eventually faded away. A year ago, I ran into a fellow stripper DJ/comedian friend named Polo the Cholo. Polo delivered the news that Shooter had passed away. I felt genuinely sad. I felt like I lost a guardian angel.

Every kid who listened to gangster rap and watched *Scar-face* had a fantasy of becoming a glorified gangster. I was stupid enough to actually try to become one. At least now I can tell people I gave up a life of crime to become a noble comedian.

What did my parents think about me working at a strip club? I guess I'll find out after they read this book and hear about it for the first time.

CHAPTER SEVEN

HOW TO MAKE IT

S hooter still owed me some back strip club DJ wages when I left San Diego, but I was willing to forgo four hundred bucks to not confront a notorious gangster. I packed all of my worthless possessions into my two-door, four-cylinder Toyota Celica and headed back to LA. I didn't want to crawl back to my dad's apartment as a failure, and I definitely didn't want to live in that Chinese retirement community again. I'd rather try to survive on my own with the two thousand dollars I had in my college checking account. So I went on the most trusted site on the Internet, Craigslist, and found a living room for rent for three hundred bucks a month from a random dude in Hollywood. I had no idea how I was going to make it, but I was determined to never live with a bunch of old ladies talking about their periods ever again.

A couple of my comedian friends in LA told me they struck gold in the commercial acting game. My friend Will said he had done an Absolut Vodka commercial two years ago. One day of work on that commercial had made him sixty grand in residuals. *Sixty grand?! If I can just book one commercial a year, I'll be rich!* Sixty grand sounded like a million dollars to this retired strip club DJ. I made it my goal in Hollywood to become a filthy rich commercial actor. I just needed to survive on ramen noodles for six months until I booked my first commercial. It seemed like a flawlessly sound financial plan. *Pssttt, I can do this, easy!* Then I quickly realized I had to deal with the age-old question in Hollywood: *Where do I start?*

Will told me he started as an extra in that Absolut commercial, then the actor who was supposed to play the security guard in the commercial didn't show up, so the director picked the biggest (possibly fattest) extra on set and bumped him up to play the security guard as a featured actor. And boom! Sixty grand. Will told me about the infamous Central Casting office in Burbank. It's the first stop for everyone who comes off the Greyhound bus to Hollywood, where they sign up to be an extra. He also told me that if I collected three union vouchers for being an extra, then I'd be eligible to become a member of the Screen Actors Guild, the SAG union. Everyone who has ever been on-screen, from Audrey Hepburn to Brad Pitt to vodka commercial Will, is in SAG.

Wow, so you're telling me one day, if I sign up to be an extra, I can be part of SAG and go down in history with Bobby De Niro in Hollywood? That would be beyond my wildest dreams. Little did I know that there were 160,000 members in SAG and 95 percent of them were unemployed on any given day. But my ignorance outweighed my doubts, and I scurried to the Central Casting office to sign up to be a star.

Central Casting is like the open mic for actors; there's zero barrier of entry and it was filled with desperate people. Every day there are packs of people lined up to "register" to be an actor. Everyone had to grab a number and wait in a folding chair, inside of a cold gray building, just like the DMV. It was more like herding sheep than becoming an actor. You fill out some paperwork, wait for them to call your name, take a passport photo, then off you go to be a star in Hollywood. They compile a database of people who are willing to work on set for minimum wage and then they call you if they need a person to blend into the background of a commercial, TV show or movie. There are many words for extras: background actors, background artists and, my favorite, atmosphere. I quickly realized this isn't where dreams come true; it's where people sign up to be warm flesh bags that are as unnoticeable as the air in the atmosphere.

There was every type of person waiting to sign up in Central Casting, from a midwestern mom, to an authentic Montana lumberjack, to the super-good-looking dude who truly believed he was destined to be a star. It was kind of beautiful in its own way, to have a place where people who would never hang out with each other came together to pursue the same dream. But as beautiful as that might sound, realistically, only one out of a hundred thousand of us flesh bags would ever make it in this town. I'm sure this was the point where many of these people who left their lives behind for their big Hollywood dream realized, *Fuck, what am I doing here?* At least that's how I felt that day at Central Casting. I started to second-guess myself for not taking the job at Smith Barney. *Maybe I am delusional.* And just then, a dude snapped a picture of me, perfectly capturing all of my regrets in that moment. That was my first headshot in Hollywood. I was now officially signed up to be a star. Shit. I went home, and by home, I mean a random Craigslist guy's living room with my twin-size mattress.

Random Craigslist guy was a twenty-year-old black dude named Nathan, but he insisted people call him Nathaniel. He was smaller than me but had twice the pizzazz, a gay man having the time of his life in Hollywood. I never figured out what he did for a living, but he somehow managed to rent this apartment and throw the occasional party. One night he invited his buddies, five gay Latino dudes to be exact, to the apartment for a little get-together. They seemed like nice, friendly dudes, and I mostly kept myself occupied playing *Halo* on the Xbox. What Nathaniel didn't tell me was that all five of his fabulous Latino hunks planned on crashing in the apartment that night, and he could only accommodate one of them in his room, because, well, Nathaniel believed in monogamy. The other four dudes would crash in the living room with me. Whatever. I guess I'd finally have my first all-American slumber party.

It was three in the morning, I lay down on my bed, but all of them were still taking tequila shots. Then two of them started making out right next to my head, and the other two were egging them on. I kept my eyes closed, pretending to be asleep. Then I kept hearing one dude repeatedly say, "Hey, Pablo, you're a power bottom, huh?" For people who don't know what a power bottom is, I'm not going to explain it in this book; just google it on UrbanDictionary.com. Look, I love gay people, but if anyone, gay or straight, starts talking about taking it up the ass next to me when I sleep, I'm right to feel a little uncomfortable. I didn't want to know what was going to happen beyond this point, so I kept my eyes closed, put on my headphones and started blasting Jay-Z at max volume. Till today, I have no idea what exactly happened that night. All I know is there were four dudes with perfectly trimmed eyebrows next to me and one of them was a power bottom. By the time I woke up, nobody was there anymore. *Maybe it was all a dream?* It was definitely all a dream. Right?

There were a lot of things I chose to not understand when I lived with Nathaniel. The second month I was there, he had trouble coming up with his eight-hundred-dollar share of the rent. I had already given him my precious three hundred dollars, so this was beyond frustrating. *What if he takes my three hundred bucks and we still both get evicted? That's bullshit!* When I asked him, "Hey, are you going to be able to come up with your rent?" he would just brush me off and say, "Don't worry about it, I'll get it." I tried my best to not worry about getting evicted and prayed that Pablo or his four friends would loan him some money.

It was now the twentieth of the month, the landlord had already come and knocked on our door twice and I was sure the third time was going to be the end. I was about to either be homeless or institutionalized in the old Chinese people community. I was stressing out so badly, no amount of *Halo* or Jay-Z could distract me. And Nathaniel was just chilling in his room without a care in the world. Then around four o'clock in the afternoon there was a knock on the door. I turned off the TV and jumped under my covers, pretending nobody was home.

"Coming!" said Nathaniel, as he casually cruised out of his room.

"What the fuck are you doing? Don't answer that!" I whispered.

"It's okay, it's my friend."

Nathaniel opened the door. It wasn't the landlord. On the other side of the door was a sheepish seventy-year-old gray-haired man wearing a cashmere cardigan sweater. They didn't greet each other or even shake hands. Nathaniel led him to his room without saying a word. He shut the door behind him and locked it. And once again, I chose to remain ignorant and put on my headphones to Jay-Z's *Black Album*. Ten minutes later, the old man strolled out of Nathaniel's room and left without ever making eye contact with me. I had no idea what happened in that room that day. All I know is Nathaniel had the rent money after that and I wasn't evicted.

I couldn't even land a job as an extra. I'd call in to the Central Casting system every day, where there was a prerecorded message for available extra work. If there was something that fit your look, you would call another number to put your name and headshot in for approval. I called in for "college background kids" and "Chinatown teenagers" several times, but for some reason I'd never get a response. Maybe they saw the deep regret in my headshot OR maybe I was too good looking to blend in with the atmosphere. I'm sure they thought if I was in a background of a TV show, the audience would be so distracted by my beauty, they couldn't concentrate on the show. "Oh my God, who is that kid in the background eating a sandwich? He's way too hot, I can't even pay attention to the show!" Well, at least that's the story I tried to tell myself of in order to preserve what little ego I had left.

A few months went by and I'd made zero dollars and no progress in LA. I was just hanging out at open mics with zero prospects and my strip club savings were running thin. A friend who worked at the Comedy Store suggested I sign up on the casting websites. Casting websites such as LACasting.com and ActorsAccess.com give actors opportunities to submit for acting jobs themselves, without representation. Usually, these jobs are shabby nonunion reenactment gigs like *America's Most Wanted* that pay a hundred dollars to play a serial murderer on the loose. I didn't mind working those jobs and I desperately needed that hundred bucks, but the problem was none of them ever really fit my description. I mean, when was the last time you saw an Asian murderer on *America's Most Wanted*? But what the hell, I didn't have anything else going on, so I gave it a shot. I signed up for a membership on all the casting websites. It was as desperate as a divorcée signing up for all the dating websites on the Internet in search of a new lover. None of these casting sites was free. They were all part of a racket to make money off of people's dreams in Hollywood. It cost fifteen dollars a month to be a member, thirty dollars to upload a headshot and forty dollars to upload an acting reel on each website. I couldn't afford new headshots, which would have cost a cool five hundred dollars, so I had my friend take some amateur headshots of my hair blowing in the wind. I didn't have an acting reel. How was I supposed to have an acting reel if I'd never acted before? So I just put up two minutes of my stand-up comedy video. I checked off all the special skills on the websites' digital résumés. I thought if someone was willing to pay me, I could always learn to ride a unicycle and wrangle some ferrets. On LACasting.com, there's an "additional skill set" comment box, and I wrote "New in town, good comedic timing, looking for representation." It was a desperate cry for help.

A week later, I got an email from a talent agency that wanted to meet with me and potentially sign me as a client. *Huzzah! Someone has finally discovered my talent! The gamble paid off and I AM destined to be a star!* I went down to the local printer and printed out ten copies of my eight-by-ten headshot, and I was on my way to meet with my first Hollywood agent. I was nervous. I knew this could make or break my career.

I pulled up to the agency's address in my Celica and it was an apartment building in Santa Monica. I double-checked my email hoping I had the wrong zip code, but this was it, a two-story apartment building. I took a peek inside and I saw a clipboard that said "Commercial Agency, sign in here." *Maybe this is a personal interview at the agent's home!* I put down my name and I sat quietly in the empty lobby. I waited anxiously for twenty minutes; my legs were shaking as I wiped the sweat from my palms on my pants. Then I heard a lady call out, "Jimmy?" I perked up.

"Yes, that's me!" She gave me a warm smile and said, "Follow me, please." She led me down the hallway and we walked right past the elevators. Every step we took away from the elevators, I became more concerned that I was going to be sold to a human trafficking ring. When we reached the end of the hallway, she opened a door in front of me and said, "Welcome." And there I was. The agency was inside of a fucking rental office.

It was a small room filled with Ikea office furniture. There was an adjustable desk in the middle of the space; it was $69.99 from Ikea. I knew this because I had taken note of the wooden top with metal legs when I went there last week looking for the cheapest desk I could find. Sitting behind the desk was a stern bald man with glasses. He flatly greeted me without making any eye contact. "Hello." And before I could reply, he handed me a small piece of paper and said, "Can you read this for me?" I looked down and I started reading:

> "Staples, where everything you need for back to school
> is in one—"
> "Can you read that to the camera?" the man behind
> the Ikea desk cut me off.

I looked up and the lady who led me in was now holding a small Toshiba home video camcorder. She said:

> "Slate your name please."
> "What?"
> "Just slate your name to the camera."

I had no idea what that meant. I froze. And she looked at me exactly how the "What's up?" girl from middle school looked at me. She wasn't sure if I was deaf or dumb or both. She kept her patience and explained, "Slating your name means saying your name to the camera; just introduce yourself." *Why the fuck didn't you just say that then? What the fuck is a slate?* I concealed my rage and followed her instructions like a good boy.

"Hi, my name is Jimmy, I am originally from Hong Kong, now I live—"
"Just your name is fine," the Ikea desk man cut me off again. "Now read your sides."

I had no idea what sides were either, but instead of freezing up again, I assumed it was the generic Staples commercial he handed me, so I started:

"Staples, where everything you need for back to school is in one store. Staples, make more happen."
"Okay, thanks."

And that was it. The lady put the camcorder down and ushered me out of the rental office / agency. *Well, I blew it.* I blew my shot in Hollywood because I didn't know what *slate* meant. My barrier with the English language had come back to knock me down in the most important interview of my life. All my English training and watching BET *Rap City* meant nothing. I sucked so bad I was rejected by a commercial agency in an apartment rental office. Time to call it quits and move back to my dad's. It was stupid of me to think that I could make it as anything in Hollywood; I was obviously destined to be a quiet financial adviser like the nice Asian boy my dad wanted me to be.

I wallowed under the covers on my twin-size mattress for the next few days as my self-loathing took over. I got a call to do a stand-up gig in Paso Robles, a desert wine town in the middle of nowhere in California. It was four hours away for a fifty-dollar paycheck. So I hopped into my Celica and journeyed to briefly escape from my grim reality in LA. The show was in a bar converted from a barn; it smelled like whiskey and cow shit. I was asked to do twenty-five minutes but I really only had fifteen minutes of material at the time. Ten extra minutes onstage doesn't sound that long, but that's a lifetime when you run out of material. It's like being on a first date and completely running out of things to say, so you sit there twiddling your thumbs wanting to kill yourself, except instead of one girl judging you, it's a hundred drunk people judging you on a brightly lit stage. But hey, I needed those fifty bucks to upload a couple more headshots on LACasting.com.

I went onstage and the drunken crowd wasn't very interested in seeing what this no-name comedian had to say. They just wanted to drink and they'd honestly prefer some music from the jukebox than a live comedian. I got some chuckles here and there, but none of the jokes really hit; half of the crowd was talking over me and the other half was busy ordering drinks from the bar. I got through all of my material in twenty minutes, and now I had to attempt to do some crowd work for another five.

"So how long have you guys been together?" I asked a couple in the front row.

Silence.

"Where did you guys meet?"

Nothing.

"Was it the grocery store? You guys look like a grocery store couple."

"No."

It was bad, but I got through it without anyone throwing a glass or screaming racial slurs at me. Luckily, I got my pay in cash and the bar manager was sympathetic enough to offer me a free meal. I accepted a nine-dollar cheeseburger, so my payments came out to a total of $59.88, if you include the tax on the cheeseburger. After spending thirty dollars on gas, I got out of Dodge with twenty dollars in my pocket and nine dollars in my stomach. All that just to live another day in LA; maybe I should quit comedy and start doing what Nathaniel did to that old man.

The next morning, I had another agency appointment from LACasting.com. I was exhausted from the eight-hour round trip from the night before, and I didn't know if my body could physically take any more shaming. I would have stabbed myself with a samurai sword and ritually *seppukued* myself if I was rejected by another apartment rental office agency. This agency was all the way in Torrance, about an hour south of Hollywood. My appointment was at 10:00 A.M. and I didn't even bother setting an alarm to wake up for it. I was woken up by Nathaniel and his hot Latin lover friend making coffee at eight, and as much as I wanted to, I just couldn't go back to sleep. I rolled around in my mattress for a while and Nathaniel asked:

"What you got going today?"
"Nothing, I have another stupid agency meeting, but I don't think I'm gonna go. It's all the way in fucking Torrance."
"You should go. What do you have to lose?"

Nathaniel was probably trying to get me out of the house so he could get some alone time with his hot Latin lover, but he was right. *I just drove four hours for a fifty-dollar gig in a barn and I think I'm too good to meet with an agent?* I pulled myself together and headed for Torrance.

I wanted to turn around during every minute of that hour-long drive. The whole time I was praying I wouldn't pull up to another apartment complex. I would have cried and crashed my car into the rental office. Luckily, I found myself at a nicely gated office building with a legitimate security guard. Instead of a sign-up sheet in the apartment lobby, I had to show my driver's license to get into the building.

"Your name is not in the system," the security guard told me.
"My name is Man Shing on my license but I go by Jimmy."
"Okay, Jimmy, elevator to your right."

Yes! I get to use the elevator this time! I went upstairs and I was greeted by an actual receptionist!

"Hi, I'm here to see Jane at Vesta Talent Agency? My name is Jimmy."
"Jane will be right with you."

As standard as that exchange might have seemed, it was a positive one-eighty from the previous nightmare experience. This time, I wasn't nervous at all; I expected nothing and I had nothing to lose, not even my pride. I guess it was pretty liberating to hit rock bottom. I waited for a few minutes and a woman wearing a perfectly pressed pantsuit came out to greet me. "Hi, Jimmy? I'm Jane, pleasure to meet you." She seemed professional and she didn't hand me a slip of paper with a Staples commercial on it. I was already sold. Jane was a skinny woman who carried a charming smile on her face, but at the same time, there was also a deep intensity about her. We sat down in an empty conference room and she told me Vesta Talent was a one-woman boutique agency and she used to be an actress from Julliard. Whenever she wasn't smiling, she stared deep into my eyes with intent; you could tell she used to be a good actress and now she was a fierce agent. She called Vesta Talent the "Ivy League agency." I was impressed, but it didn't take much to wow this beginner who bombed an audition in front of an Ikea desk. She said to me, "I think you have a good look." I later learned that having a "good look" is quite different than being good looking. In Hollywood, having a good look means a person fits into a certain type, whether it's a heroin addict, an Italian mob boss or a nerdy college student. Ryan

Gosling is good looking; Luis Guzmán and I have a good look. Then Jane said, "Think about it, and let me know." "Let's do it," I replied without any hesitation. Since I had nothing else going on, I didn't need to think about it at all. And that's how I got my first agent in Hollywood.

Jane wasn't wrong about me having a good look; a week after signing with Vesta Talent, the auditions started to come in. Some of them were small regional commercials and others were big-time shows that were far beyond my expectations. One of my first auditions was for a part on *Modern Family*. Getting that audition email notice was surreal to me. I was just hoping to get an audition for a TGI Fridays commercial, but I was now thrown into the mix for some real acting. I wasn't prepared for any of this. I didn't even know what slate meant two weeks ago. How was I supposed to nail this big-time *Modern Family* audition?

The role was Haley's new friend from school who was a weed dealer. Perfect, I knew all the weed I'd smoked in college would eventually pay off. They clearly wanted an Asian actor for this role. The waiting room was filled with every single Asian person in LA. They called my name and I was ushered into an unassuming office. Sitting across from me was just one man, no assistants, no camcorders. He was a small middle-aged man who wore a polo shirt a size too small, but somehow it looked right on him. It was the legendary Jeff Greenberg. He was responsible for casting such mega hits as *Cheers, Wings* and *Frasier,* and now he was ready to discover the next Bruce Lee. Before I could close the door behind me, Jeff cut to the chase: "Are you ready? I'll read with you." I snapped my head around. "Sure, I'm ready." I wasn't. I stumbled through the scene and stood still in front of him. I looked at him like a puppy begging for a treat. I was eager for a compliment, which was the desperate actor's ultimate treat. He thought for a second and said:

"Okay, let's do it again. This character is genuine, he's actually a nice kid, play that."

"Got it. So he's like not lying to her?" I asked.

"Jesus Christ! Just do what I told you!" out of nowhere, Jeff exploded.

I felt like a musket shot me in the face, and my self-esteem was bleeding out. Did I do something wrong? Was I not supposed to ask questions in an audition? Did he not like the shape of my forehead? I had a million questions of doubt for myself. And before I could snap out of my downward spiral, Jeff started reading the scene again. I blurted out what I could with my face down on the sides. I would have cried at that moment, but I wasn't even a good enough actor to produce tears in real life. Needless to say, I never heard back from Jeff and *Modern Family* again. The little bit of confidence I had left crawled out of my body. I still can't watch *Modern Family* to this day; it's like a Vietnam War veteran eating at a pho restaurant.

I went to college for economics; the only acting experience I ever had was lying to my dad about knowing algebra in middle school. I didn't know the first thing about acting. *Who is Stella Adler? What is a* Street Car Named Desire? All I knew was Arnold in *True Lies*. Everyone else at these auditions seemed to have come from a legitimate acting school and a lifetime of theater. I was just a comedian telling jokes at a barn. I desperately needed to take some acting classes, except the acting classes were more expensive than my rent. But I had no choice; once again, I had to pay into the Hollywood racket for dreamers. I traded in two months' worth of rent money to sign up for my very first acting class. I was paying six hundred dollars a month for acting class while living in a three-hundred-dollar-a-month living room. I had sixty days to learn how to act and book my first gig, before my bank account hit zero.

Two months of acting classes and ten auditions later, I still hadn't come close to booking a job. I bombed every audition. I had four packs of ramen left to my name. Then I received an audition email for the part of a "Person in Line" on a new sitcom called *2 Broke Girls,* and it could very well be my last before I gave in to a life of prostitution. It was a two-line part as the name would imply, and there was no specific character description. He or she was simply an impatient, angry person in line at a grocery store, complaining about how slow the line was moving. They weren't specifically looking for an Asian person, a young person or even a dude. Anyone could have qualified for this role. I wasn't just competing with other Asians this time. As small as the role was, I had to compete with every kind of actor in town for it. The odds against me were pretty grim.

It was rush hour on a Tuesday in Hollywood. Traffic was awful and I got to the audition ten minutes late. The only parking spot I found was five blocks away from the audition. Instead of trying to find a closer spot, which is a near impossible feat in Hollywood, I got out of my car and sprinted up Sunset Boulevard faster than Forrest Gump. By the time I got to the building, I was a full thirty minutes behind the scheduled appointment. I hopped up the two flights of stairs and shuffled into the lobby panting heavily, with my forehead completely drenched in sweat. The waiting room was eerily empty. I looked at the sign-up sheet and every name had already been checked off. I was too late. I looked up to see the casting director walking out of the audition room with her purse, headed for the exit. She saw me and called out to her associate, "Hey, Joey, we got one more." She turned to me with a smile and said, "Have fun." This was the wonderful Julie Ashton, who was responsible for casting one of my favorite shows, *MADtv*. I trudged into the audition room; Joey was ready with a camcorder.

"Slate your name."
I did, flawlessly this time.
Then he asked, "Do you have any questions?"
"Nope." I knew better after what happened at Jeff Greenberg's office.

I wiped the sweat from my forehead and took a deep breath; I was so flustered, I forgot how to be nervous. Then I let out all my pent-up frustration from Central Casting, the apartment rental agency and *Modern Family* in those two lines on the sides. "Hey, come on! Hurry up! I'll buy it for you!" Those would eventually become my first lines on TV.

When Jane called me next morning, "Congratulations! You booked it!" I felt like I had won the lottery. I called all my friends to brag about the news, and I'm sure I posted some cheesy humble brag post on Facebook. "Finally, after all the sweat and tears, I've booked a role on TV! If you believe in yourself, you can too!

But for now, everybody look at me while I humble brag on social media!" I told my parents about the good news, but I didn't expect much of a reaction from them. My dad asked, "So how much does it pay?" And my mom, to this day, still calls the show *"2 Broken Girls."* To be honest, that doesn't sound like a bad show; I can see it on HBO starring Kristen Stewart and Chlöe Moretz.

I made my television debut on *2 Broke Girls* on CBS prime time. This qualified me to join the Screen Actors Guild without collecting the three vouchers from Central Casting. It's a straight-to-union rule called Taft-Hartley that every new actor dreams about. I truly felt like I'd made it. It might not have paid as much as Will's vodka commercial, but it gave me the money to keep going for another two months, and more importantly, it reinstated my confidence. When the episode finally aired, I called everyone I knew to tune in to CBS at 9:00 P.M. My dad said, "I don't have CBS." And that was the end of the phone call. *Who the fuck doesn't have CBS?* You can stick a piece of tin foil in the back of the TV and get CBS. Dad was just a hater. He eventually called back and said he'd come and watch the episode with me. It might not have been a Nobel Prize, but I did see a smile from my dad when my name came up in the credits.

THREE DUDES, ONE ROOM

I finally moved out of Nathaniel's apartment when Tarrell from the Comedy Palace decided to move up to LA. Tarrell and I rented a one-bedroom apartment in the Little Armenia neighborhood in East Los Angeles, where the only landmarks were an Armenian vacuum repair shop and a Scientology center. It definitely wasn't the posh part of town. I'd sleep in the living room while Tarrell paid an extra hundred dollars for the bedroom. Then two weeks later, my bank account was hit with an overdraft fee for insufficient funds. I guess the *2 Broke Girls* money didn't last as long as I thought. Then I looked at my bank statements and saw there was a thirteen-hundred-dollar check that bounced. I didn't remember writing such a check; I mean at that time thirteen hundred dollars was an astronomical figure and I wouldn't forget writing that check. So I went to the bank and asked for a copy of this mystery check. It had a poorly forged signature of mine, and it was made out to none other than Nathaniel. That son of a bitch stole one of my blank checks before I left and had the balls to make it out to himself. How stupid and desperate do you have to be to literally write your own name on a very illegal stolen check? Luckily, I was so poor I didn't have thirteen hundred dollars in my bank account, so the check bounced and my account was frozen. I went down to the Hollywood police station and reported it to an officer: "My old roommate committed check fraud. He stole my check and made it out to his name. Here's the evidence." I handed him the copy of the fraudulent check, hard evidence.

The officer asked:

"So he stole thirteen hundred dollars from you?"
"He tried to steal thirteen hundred dollars from me, but it didn't work."
"So he didn't really steal from you."
"He stole my check and forged my signature!"

"Well, if he didn't technically steal anything from you, we can't really charge him on anything substantial."

I thought about taking matters into my own hands and going back to Nathaniel's apartment to kick his ass. But I thought better of it; I didn't want to be the one who ended up getting arrested. The bank eventually waived the thirty-five-dollar overdraft fee and unfroze my account, but I had completely lost faith in the LAPD.

I lived with Tarrell for a year in the Little Armenia apartment before Guam also moved in with us. We couldn't afford a bigger place, and Guam couldn't afford to pay anything because he still hadn't won the lottery yet. So we struck a deal where Guam would buy groceries for us using his EBT, government-issued food stamps, instead of paying rent. Guam slept in a ten-foot-square closet in the living room next to my bed. It was like having a pet that was a two-hundred-pound forty-year-old Guamanian man. Guam had terrible sleep apnea and snored like two elephants mating. I'd kick the closet door at four in the morning. "Guam, stop snoring." He'd startle awake for two seconds, then go right back to rumbling in the closet. I hadn't gotten a decent night's sleep since he moved in. The EBT deal didn't really work out in our favor either, because Guam ended up eating all the groceries he bought for the household. But even though we had three dudes crammed in a one-bedroom apartment, living with two of my best comedian friends was a major upgrade to living with Nathaniel the check thief. In our minds, we made it.

CHAPTER EIGHT

HOW TO SILICON VALLEY

[JIN YANG] (20s) **PLEASE SUBMIT TALENT WHO ARE _NATIVE BORN ASIAN THAT SPEAK ENGLISH_. TALENT MUST HAVE GREEN CARD OR BE US CITIZEN WITH PROPER PAPERS.** A resident at Erlich's incubator, Hacker House, Jin Yang is a tall, skinny **ASIAN** Tech geek who speaks in a <u>THICK ACCENT</u> with every other word being either s**t, f**ck, mother**ker or dude. Role slated to start shooting approx. 3/2–3/5. **POSSIBLE RECURRING GUEST STAR**

I got an audition email with this very interesting character description. It was for a new HBO pilot called *Deep Tech*, which somehow sounded too nerdy and too sexual at the same time. Jin Yang was a Chinese hacker who coded like the wind and cursed like a Cambodian pirate. The character was so foreign, they needed to make sure the actors auditioning for this character had proper paperwork. They were looking for an authentic Chinese immigrant actor who was just foreign enough to have a green card. I was born to play this role.

I threw on my gray pilly sweatpants and I slipped on a pair of ugly rubber sandals over my white socks. To complete the look, I put on an old faded T-shirt with chemical bonding diagrams that my mom had bought for me in Shanghai ten years ago. I looked like I crawled out of the back of a Chinese Internet cafe, and that was exactly how I wanted to look. I hopped into my Toyota Celica and drove to the legendary McCarthy/Abellera casting office in Santa Monica. Jeanne McCarthy and Nicole Abellera were responsible for casting classics like *Con Air*; *I, Robot*; *Eternal Sunshine of the Spotless Mind*. I was anxious to meet them for the first time. I read the sides twice and Jeanne McCarthy politely said, "Thank you." A week went by and I didn't hear from my agent. No news always means bad news when it comes to auditions.

Acting is like a never-ending job interview. You have to constantly prove yourself through the grueling audition process just to get another day of work. There are so many elements that are out of the actor's control. They could have chosen someone else for the job because I was too short, too young or too weird-looking. Acting is the only job where physical discrimination is allowed. I once auditioned for something with the character description "NO FAT PEOPLE!!!" in caps with three exclamation marks. Ironically, it was for a McDonald's chicken nuggets commercial. I never try to look for the reason why I didn't get a job; I just try to do better in the next audition. Dwelling on an audition is like dwelling on a girl who told you she's emotionally unavailable. It's best to move on or, as my agent Jane would say, "On to the next!"

Eight months and twenty-five auditions went by and I had completely forgotten about the *Deep Tech* audition. During that time, I booked a guest star role on *It's Always Sunny in Philadelphia* and a small part on *Agents of S.H.I.E.L.D.*; things seemed to be going well. All of my comedian friends thought I was killing it, popping up on different TV shows, but I felt stuck doing one-off bit parts on different shows. I felt like a foster child, getting passed around to different families, except I was an adult who had to pay rent. I was getting paid SAG-AFTRA union minimum scale, which was the lowest amount you could legally pay a union actor. It was a little over nine hundred dollars per day. That might sound like a decent payday for one day of work, but an actor would be lucky to work more than two days a year. I started to panic about my stagnant career. Making nine hundred bucks twice a year wasn't exactly the Hollywood dream I had envisioned. I'd been to more than a hundred auditions at this point, and I'd booked a total of five small guest-star roles, a couple commercials that never aired and a movie I was cut out of. I had auditioned for everything from a Chili's commercial to *Dog with a Blog. Is this going to be the rest of my life—pretending to eat buffalo wings in Chili's and auditioning to talk to a dog on a Disney kids' show?* Here is the audition log I kept:

1.	7/20/2011	Project Network	Host, Hip slacker dude host, Ethnic looking
2.	8/2/2011	Wakey Wakey	Loud Japanese host
3.	8/9/2011	Radical	Taiwanese 20, looks like 12, computer geek
4.	8/24/2011	Us & Them	Chinese restaurant owner
5.	8/24/2011	Samsung	Journalist/ DJ
6.	9/6/2011	Eagleheart	2 lines, Hipster
7.	9/14/2011	Modern Family	young Asian guy, friend of Haley
8.	9/20/2011	Sony	Interesting real blogger
9.	10/4/2011	Baby Daddy	Series Regular, Tucker, ethnic friend
10.	10/7/2011	Walmart	Walmart employee, Speaks Mandarin
11.	10/18/2011	Community	Co-star, Glee club rapper/dancer
12.	10/19/2011	How I Met your Mother	2 lines, stoner
13.	11/1/2011	Oh Henry!	Office Worker
14.	11/2/2011	Franklin & Bash	2 lines, stoner
15.	11/8/2011	2 Broke Girls	2 lines, person in line
16.	11/9/2011	Whitney	2 lines, young hipster guy
17.	12/1/2011	Target	Attractive young Bachelor
18.	12/7/2011	Retail Energy in Texas	Bad Karaoke Singer
19.	12/9/2011	Chevy Malibu	Chinese driver, a young Tony Leung
20.	12/9/2011	Coca-Cola	Young, Attractive Chinese
21.	12/16/2011	Sprite	Chinese speaking DJ
22.	1/5/2012	McDonald's	Asian artist, painter
23.	2/2/2012	Rocket Ship China	Hip, attractive Chinese boy
24.	2/3/2012	Banshee	Series Regular, kick ass computer hacker Tranny
25.	2/10/2012	Admissions	College Roomate, supporting, Andy Garcia indy film
26.	2/10/2012	BFF	Nerd, harry potter guy
27.	2/15/2012	Undateable	Series Regular, young pissed off guy
28.	2/21/2012	Toyota	Young Taco stand patron
29.	2/23/2012	Friend Me	Young Ethnic, poker player
30.	3/6/2012	In Living Color	Characters and Impressions

31.	3/21/2012	TW Cable	High School twilight fan
32.	3/21/2012	Modelo	All types beer commercial
33.	3/23/2012	TW Cable	High School twilight fan
34.	4/9/2012	Johnson	Young man, faithful to his girl
35.	4/11/2012	Chavez	Day Player, Filipino/Chinese workers
36.	5/4/2012	Liberty Mutual	Driver
37.	5/4/2012	Bunheads	Skinny mechanic
38.	5/10/2012	Nissan Altima	Husband
39.	5/10/2012	The Internship	computer geek
40.	5/25/2012	Bunheads	Recurring, cute high school boyfriend
41.	6/6/2012	Workaholics	2 lines, college kid
42.	6/7/2012	Go Daddy	awkward techie nerd
43.	6/13/2012	Microsoft	Young record executive, hip
44.	6/13/2012	Bunheads	Guest Star, young usher
45.	6/18/2012	Good Luck Charlie	2 lines, college kid
46.	6/20/2012	Volvo	Chinese Brothers
47.	6/20/2012	The Internship	Chinese Ping Pong Player
48.	6/21/2012	A Leading Man	Supporting, Chinese surfer guy
49.	7/6/2012	Samsung	Hip/Casual
50.	8/1/2012	Arrested Development	Recurring, Super Secretive, cold read
51.	8/20/2012	Crash And Bernstein	Recurring, Stoner Kid
52.	8/23/2012	Catonese Demo	Cantonese
53.	9/10/2012	T-Mobile	Band Guy, good comedic timing/good actor
54.	9/20/2012	Toyota	Hipster
55.	10/1/2012	Goodwin Games	2 lines
56.	10/1/2012	Western Digital	Speak Cantonese
57.	10/9/2012	Marvin Marvin	2 lines, pissed off customer
58.	10/11/2012	Ford Fusion	Physical Improv, feat. Garfunkel & Oates
59.	10/22/2012	God's Not Dead	Lead, Speak Chinese, Accent
60.	10/31/2012	Nike	Speak Mandarin, riding a bike (hip)

61.	11/6/2012	McDonald's	Guy eating chicken nuggets
62.	11/7/2012	Full House 2	Plays violin, full concert attire
63.	11/15/2012	Need for Speed	Supporting, Computer whiz, friendly, sincere
64.	1/5/2013	McDonald's	Sports Fan
65.	1/14/2013	Apple	Voice of Siri, in Mandarin
66.	1/16/2013	Larry Gaye	3 lines, lab tech
67.	1/24/2013	America's Got Talent	Private audish, 90 sec standup
68.	1/28/2013	Castle	stoner PO Box guy, 4 lines
69.	1/29/2013	Happy Endings	2 lines, nice hair guy
70.	1/30/2013	Verizon	Proud son, a lot of dialogue
71.	2/11/2013	Good Luck Charlie	Nerd, chess club
72.	2/20/2013	The Mindy Project	Asian Video Game addict
73.	2/22/2013	Revenge of Green Dragons	Movie, Chinese Gangster
74.	2/27/2013	Chilli's	Buddy/Neighbor
75.	2/27/2013	Deep Tech	Computer Programmer
76.	3/8/2013	Infamous 3 VO	Video Game, Chinese Pedestrian
77.	4/10/2013	The Gateway	Asian nephew, soft but wanna-be gangster type
78.	4/12/2013	Verizon	Hipster intern
79.	5/8/2013	Always Sunny	Lab tech, Chinese accent, Mandarin, guest star
80.	6/5/2013	Me Him Her	Weird Korean Jogger guy
81.	6/5/2013	The Walking Dead	Jack, stoner, teenager, meets his girl
82.	6/28/2013	Hello Ladies	Camera Guy/ Ronnie, wangster street guy
83.	7/2/2013	Scion	Hipster guy
84.	7/11/2013	Wayward Pines	Assistant secret service agent, eager, comic relief
85.	7/18/2013	Two and a Half Men	Seeking a job as assistant to Walden Schmidt
86.	7/22/2013	Shlub Life	Punk ass high school kid
87.	7/27/2013	Subway	sandwich artist
88.	7/29/2013	NBC Sketch Pilot	Sketch, characters
89.	7/30/2013	Alexander and the Terrible...	2 lines, Young Asian tech boss
90.	8/22/2013	Lenovo	Rock band member

91.	8/22/2013	Wonder Years	Older teen boy
92.	8/27/2013	Agents of SHIELD	Chinese teenager
93.	8/30/2013	Sean Saves the World	2 lines, IT call center, all ethnicity
94.	9/10/2013	NBC Scene Showcase	2 different scenes from comedy shows
95.	9/24/2013	Brooklyn Nine-Nine	Korean Hacker guy, early 20s with British accent
96.	10/15/2013	Coca-Cola	Authentic Asian family. Mom and Dad came too. Awesome
97.	10/18/2013	Hawaii Five-O	young Asian/Hawaiian Thug
98.	10/18/2013	Mixology	Fun party guy
99.	10/21/2013	Hot in Cleveland	uptight lawyer guy, giving a restraining order
100.	10/22/2013	Mappers	Asian high schooler
101.	10/25/2013	The Rebels	2 lines, High school kid

For my 102nd audition, I got another email from Jeanne Mc-Carthy's casting office. It was once again for the role of Jian Yang, now spelled with an *a* in *Jin*, and the show had changed its name from *Deep Tech* to *Silicon Valley*. *Silicon Valley* was already in production and this Jian Yang character had become a smaller two-line part in episode three. I later learned the original pilot was never shot and the script was completely rewritten. Not booking that first audition had nothing to do with me at all: the original Jin Yang was written out of the pilot in the process. It was like finding out your crush rejected you because she was actually a lesbian. I felt slightly better about myself.

I strolled into the McCarthy/Abellera casting office once again in my same sandals over socks, gray sweatpants and awkward chemistry T-shirt combo.

"This is Pied Piper."

"Yes, this, here. Pied Piper."

Two lines, one take, that was it. I read it on tape for Leslie Woo, one of the casting associates at Jeanne's office who would later become a top casting director. Leslie said, "Thank you" and once again I drove home in my frumpy sweatpants. "On to the next!" I couldn't tell you what I had for breakfast that day, or what I did after the audition, because I thought it was just another day. There was no callback or screen test after that audition, which is common for a part that small. The casting directors can't waste their time calling back every little part on the show; usually the producers cast straight off of the audition videotapes.

Two days later, I got a call from Jane. "You got the part! It shoots for one day and it pays scale." And that's how I became Jian Yang. I was happy to make another nine hundred bucks, but there was something special about this two-line part. The creator of *Silicon Valley* was also the creator of *Beavis and Butt-Head,* my commencement speaker at UCSD, Mike Judge. When I was sitting in the audience as a hungover college student listening to that commencement speech, I had no idea I would become an actor; I was an economics major destined to be a miserable desk jockey. Five years later, I was at a table read, sitting across from the man who inspired me to pursue my dreams.

I EAT THE FISH

The table read took place at an unassuming conference room at the Culver Studios. I sat across from Mike Judge, the other producers, writers and the cast. I knew of Kumail Nanjiani and T. J. Miller from the stand-up world. They were the guys who I'd looked up to, both having been series regulars on other TV shows and had their Comedy Central spots. I'd seen Zach Woods and Martin Starr in *The Office* and *The 40-Year-Old Virgin* and it was the first time I'd seen Thomas Middleditch, who played the lead role of Richard Hendricks. Nobody had heard of *Silicon Valley* yet, but each of them painted such a vivid picture of their distinct characters. There was an undeniable chemistry between the five of them that shone through with every written line and improvisation. They riffed off of each other even at the table read and they never missed a beat. It seemed like they had been doing this show for ten seasons.

Next to me was the late, great Christopher Evan Welch. The man was a master-class actor. I learned so much about comedy just from watching him at the table read. He portrayed the eccentric billionaire investor Peter Gregory. It was the first time I learned how silence could be just as funny as any sharply constructed joke:

"Have any of you . . ." Christopher pauses for a beat.
". . . ever eaten at Burger King?"
"Yes, why?" his business associate responds.
"Well . . ." He takes it in, as we eagerly anticipate his next words. "I was just driving past one. And while I know

their market cap is seven-plus billion dollars I realize I am unfamiliar with their offerings."

"You've never eaten at Burger King? Okay, but what does—"

Christopher swiftly cuts him off: "Is it popular among your peer group? Is it . . ." He stares at his associate for half a beat. ". . . enjoyed?"

He put pauses in places you wouldn't expect and he gave every sentence a distinct rhythm. His cadence drew just as much laughs as the lines. Christopher was like a maestro conducting an orchestra of words. It was truly amazing.

I briefly met all the cast and producers after the read. Even though I only had two lines, everybody treated me like I was part of the family. Thinking this was my first and last chance, I went up to Mike Judge and introduced myself.

"Hey, Mike, I'm Jimmy. You were my commencement speaker at UCSD."

"Really?" Mike was pleasantly surprised. "How was UCSD when you went there?"

"Super fucking boring. I hated it," I blurted out how I really felt. Luckily, he laughed.

I usually get pretty nervous when I get on set. I am nervous I'll botch the lines, I am nervous I haven't done enough homework on the character and I am nervous people will discover I am an economics major trying to fake his way into being an actor. But something felt very natural about being Jian Yang. It was as if I'd been playing him for years. I felt like I was playing an earlier version of myself.

For my very first take on *Silicon Valley*, I sleepily shuffled down the hallway to answer the door at the Hacker House. I opened the door to an angry man who was looking for my roommates, Thomas, Zach and Kumail, who were hiding from him around the corner.

"Do you know where Pied Piper is?" the angry man asked.

"This is Pied Piper," I, Jian Yang, replied, matter-of-factly.

"This is Pied Piper?"

"Yes, this, here. Pied Piper."

Then Kumail's character, Dinesh, tripped over a lamp and the gang was busted. The angry man marched in, determined to kick their ass. Zach's character, Jared, said earlier in the episode: "If you repeatedly scream your name, it forces the assailant to acknowledge you as a human being." The nervous Richard would repeatedly blurt out his own name while Dinesh would say Gilfoyle's (Martin's) name to try to frame him; and Jared would innocently say his real name, Donald. It was a masterfully written bit where three different jokes landed at once, and it perfectly showcased the personalities of each character.

There wasn't a particular gag for Jian Yang; I was supposed to just stand there in confusion. I thought to myself, *What would*

Jian Yang do? Which translated to *What would I have done when I first came to America?* I thought it would make sense for Jian Yang to follow the lead of his American peers, thinking it was an American custom to repeat your name when a guest arrives. It was like what I did in my first day of school in America in eighth grade, when I followed everyone's lead to recite the Pledge of Allegiance. I had no idea why everyone was doing it, but I followed the lead anyway. So I took a chance in the second take and decided to repeat my name with the rest of the gang: "Jian Yang, Jian Yang, Jian Yang."

That was the take that made the cut. It always feels great when an improvised moment makes it on the screen. But it felt even more satisfying to leave a part of my immigrant experience on the screen. I *was* a lost and confused immigrant like Jian Yang.

When we wrapped that day, I was sad that this would be the first and last time I got to be Jian Yang and work with these hilarious people. When I packed up my bag and left my trailer, Zach Woods came up to me.

"Really funny stuff today, man," Zach said in his always genuine tone.

"Thanks! It was so fun to get to work with you guys."

"Have you seen your other stuff coming up?"

"What?" I had no idea what he was referring to.

"Yeah, you have another really funny scene coming up."

"Really!?" I almost shrieked. This was amazing news to me.

It turned out the scene Zach was referring to was the "I Eat the Fish" scene in the following episode. I was stoked that I would work another day at scale for another nine hundred bucks, but more importantly, I got to be Jian Yang again. I was over the moon.

The "I Eat the Fish" scene would be the first time I worked with T. J. Miller and his character, Erlich Bachman. Something about our difference in size and mannerisms just instantly clicked. There was something naturally funny about the juxtaposition of a small deadpan Jian Yang and a large loudmouthed Erlich. Mike Judge came up to me between takes and gave me one simple note: "Before you say your first line, can you stand still and don't say anything for a few seconds?" In the next take, I stood still and stared up at TJ for a good five seconds, re-creating the same confused look I gave to the girl in eighth grade who said, "What's up?" to me. Then I slowly uttered, "Yes, I eat the fish." The crew cracked up. "I eat the fish" became one of the most popular lines from Jian Yang. People still scream that out to me in public: "Hey! You're the 'I eat the fish' guy!" To which I always respond, "What's up?"

JIAN YANG: UBER DRIVER

I guest starred in a total of three episodes on the first season of *Silicon Valley*. I was paid a grand total of twenty-seven hundred dollars. I invested the money as a down payment for a used 2006 Prius, so I could drive Uber. As the old saying goes, "Give a man an acting job, you feed him for a day; teach a man to Uber, you feed him for a lifetime." I was still sleeping in the living room of the one-bedroom apartment with Tarrell occupying the bedroom and Guam quartered in my closet. Not much had changed. We still couldn't afford to go to Red Lobster. I was hoping *Silicon Valley* would bring me back for season two, but I surely didn't count on it. I drove Uber eight hours a day, and went to auditions and acting classes in between customers. I once fired up my Uber Driver app after leaving my acting class and I was matched to pick up one of my classmates. To make matters worse, it was the pretty girl I had a crush on. Then just as I was pulling up, the trip was canceled for some reason. So I rolled down my window and asked:

"Hey, Jessica, did you call an Uber?"

"Yeah, but I canceled it. My boyfriend's coming to pick me up."

I wanted to drive my Prius off of a cliff.

Four months and a hundred Uber trips later, I received an audition email from Wendy O'Brien's casting office, which had cast me on *It's Always Sunny in Philadelphia* before. Wendy and her partner, Jeff, are two of the kindest casting directors and have championed me since day one. They believed in me before I believed in myself. This was a callback audition for a new Yahoo series called *Sin City Saints*. The show was about a fictional expansion basketball team in Las Vegas. It was one of the first original series from Yahoo, an attempt to position itself as a new streaming platform like Netflix. The audition was for a series-regular role on *Sin City Saints*. This was a big deal. Being a series regular would surely be the big break in my acting career. The difference between a guest star and a series regular is the difference between driving UberX and taking UberBlack. My friend Fred Stoller, a longtime character actor, who guest starred as Raymond's cousin in *Everybody Loves Raymond,* said it best: "You know what the difference is between playing Raymond's cousin and Raymond's brother on the show? About forty million dollars." Brad Garrett was the series regular that played Raymond's brother on the syndicated sitcom. Fred is also the author of the great book *Maybe We'll Have You Back: The Life of a Perennial TV Guest Star.* As someone who was also passed around guest starring in different shows like an unwanted foster child, this book resonated with me. I dropped off an Uber customer and drove to Wendy's casting office with a potential forty million dollars at stake.

The character was named Byron Summers. Byron was a basketball statistician much like Jonah Hill in *Moneyball.* The character was written to be African American. I had to go in and change their minds. Two black actors and I waited outside of the audition room at Wendy O'Brien's office. I thought to myself, *Shit. They are definitely looking for a black dude. Doesn't matter how much BET I've watched, I have no chance.* But I stayed focused, knowing that getting this role could be the big break of my career, and it'd be a huge win for the Asian community. The pressure was on.

One by one, we went in the room to read with Wendy, Jeff and the director of the series, Bryan Gordon, who's best known for directing *Curb Your Enthusiasm.* I can always tell how well another actor is doing in an audition by how long he has been in the audition room, and my goal is always to outlast that person. When the last guy was in there for a good thirty minutes, I started to panic. *This guy must be killing it in there.* When he came out, he gave me a smirk and said, "Break a leg." I should have Tonya Harding'ed him and broken his leg right there. Then it was my turn. Wendy and Jeff gave me the usual warm welcome, but I was flustered to meet Bryan for the first time. I fumbled through the sides on the first take. The pressure of a possible forty million dollars and a billion Asian people came crashing down on me. Bryan kindly gave me some directions and asked me to do it again. I got more comfortable after every take, until I was rolling off basketball statistics like Marv Albert at the NBA finals. Next thing you know, we were all chatting in the audition room like four friends at a picnic. I looked at my watch; I had been in there for an hour. Byron Summers was about to be Chinese.

My agent, Jane, called me at eleven in the morning the next day.

"Congratulations!" she exclaimed, "you got the job! You are going to be a series regular!"

I didn't know what to say, so I just screamed. She continued, "It shoots for ten weeks in Vegas, they are going to put you up at the Caesars Palace!" I was planning to drive Uber that day, now you're telling me I get to hang out in Vegas and stay at the Caesars Palace? And get paid for it?! From the Comedy Palace to Caesars Palace. My little head couldn't even process this gigantic news. I ran around in my pajamas repeatedly screaming, "Yes! Yes! Yes!" My neighbor must have thought I was having the best sex of my life.

"But there is one thing," Jane said. "If you do this show, you can't do *Silicon Valley* anymore, because Yahoo wants you exclusively on their show."

Nothing is ever perfect, is it? I wasn't sure if I was going to be back on *Silicon Valley*, but if HBO called me to be back on the second season, I knew it was something I couldn't pass up. The first season of *Silicon Valley* was already nominated for the Emmys and Golden Globes; it was on its way to becoming a big hit. It meant everything for my career to book my first series-regular job, but how could I turn down a possible second season of an Emmy-nominated HBO show with Mike Judge? I was torn. I knew I'd make at least twenty times more money as a series regular on *Sin City Saints* than the union minimum nine hundred dollars guest starring on *Silicon Valley*. And trust me, I cared about the money. My economics degree told me, *Take the series-regular money, go to Caesars Palace.* But I ignored that econ degree the same way I did when I left Smith Barney to do stand-up. I followed my gut.

"Jane, I'd rather be a small part of a great show than a big part of an unknown show."

I put my foot down. "I really want to do *Sin City Saints,* but they need to let me do *Silicon Valley.*"

I didn't know much about the business, but I knew I couldn't give up on *Silicon Valley.* Jane's joyous tone suddenly turned heavy, but she knew I was making the right decision. "Let me call Yahoo. Let me see what I can do." When she hung up, I started second-guessing everything I'd just said. *Was that the right decision? What if I lose out on* Sin City Saints *and* Silicon Valley *doesn't call me back? Am I going to be driving Uber for eternity?* My stress level went into overdrive. I didn't know what to do, so I left my apartment and just started walking in a random direction. Twenty minutes into my stress wandering, Jane finally called back. I picked up on the first ring.

"Hello!"

"Jimmy, Yahoo wouldn't budge on the exclusivity. And they said we have until 1 P.M. to give them an answer, or else they are going to move on with somebody else."

I looked down at my watch; it was already noon. It was as if the writer of an action thriller movie wanted to heighten the stakes. There was already a bomb in Times Square, but now we discover it's a ticking time bomb that's going to blow up in twenty minutes! *Where's Bruce Willis?! I need Bruce Willis!!!*

"So what should we do?" I asked.

"Let me call HBO and see if they can match the offer."

"What do you mean?"

"I'm going to see if HBO will make you a series regular on *Silicon Valley.*"

I almost had an aneurism. *Are you crazy? There's no way!* I'm just a random schmuck who was on three episodes with five lines. We are going to look like idiots asking them to match Yahoo's series-regular offer. But I trusted Jane's seemingly outlandish idea.

"Okay." That's all I said and we hung up. Once again, I waited for her to call me back, with even more on the line this time. All the bad thoughts came crashing in again, ten times harder. *What if I burn a bridge with HBO with this crazy ask? What if Mike Judge thinks I'm an idiot? What if they kill off Jian Yang?*

With each minute that passed by, my heart rate went up by ten beats. I was on the verge of a full-blown panic attack. I was looking for anything to distract me. I walked by the farmers' market at the Grove in LA and found myself at the farmers' market bar. I sat down and ordered a beer. The only people at the farmer's market bar at noon were alcoholic degenerates who were already drunk. Everyone looked like they had been through at least two divorces and three rehabs. "Hey! Cheers!" A scraggly middle-aged man raised his glass to me. He was wasted. His downward spiral of a life flashed in front of me as if it were my own. *Fuck, is this my future self?* I pounded my beer as quickly as I could and shuffled out of that grim bar filled with cautionary tales. It was now 12:30 P.M. I wandered into the Grove's outdoor mall and saw its signature trolley pass by. It was a fancy retro trolley that took you from one side of the mall to the other, a massive waste of space, but a scenic tourist attraction. I had lived in LA for more than ten years and I'd never gone on that trolley. *Why not?* Anything to get my mind off of Yahoo and HBO. So I took a scenic seat on the top deck, sitting behind a Chinese tourist family with a little boy. I was so preoccupied with the phone calls that I didn't realize I was still wearing my pajamas. People definitely thought I was the Chinese family's degenerate elder son. The sun was blasting on the top deck and I was sweating like I was a withdrawing heroin addict. The Chinese dad glanced at me with pitiful disappointment, reminiscent of my own father. As the trolley rolled past the Cheesecake Factory, it was 12:45 P.M. *If I don't get a call in fifteen minutes, my life is over. I might as well go back to the farmers' market bar and join my peers.* Then my phone rang—Jane Schulman. That name looked like Jesus Christ My Lord and Savior to me. Before I could scream hello again, Jane said in a serious tone:

"Jimmy . . ."
She paused. My heart was about to eject out of my asshole.
"Silicon Valley is going to make you a series regular!"

Everything I'd ever worked for materialized in that sentence. Every bad audition flashed in front of me and they liquefied themselves and seeped out of my eyes as I sobbed. The weight of everything my dad expected of me lifted off of my shoulders. I sat there quietly for a moment. Then I gathered myself and screamed in the phone:

"FUCK YEAH!!!!!!!!!!"
The Chinese family in front of me shielded their kid from me and hustled off of the trolley. I screamed again into the sky:
"FUCK YEAH!!!!!!"
I knew my life was about to change.

I called my dad to share the monumental news.

"Dad, *Silicon Valley* is going to make me a series regular!"

"What is that?"

"That means I'll get paid more money, and I'll be under contract with HBO!"

"So you have a job?"

"Yeah! As a series reg—"

"Good."

He had no idea what series regular meant, but he was satisfied that I finally got a job.

HOW TO JIAN YANG

Being a series regular meant I didn't have to drive Uber anymore; it meant I could finally call myself a full-time actor. It also meant that my dad was wrong; pursuing what I loved didn't make me homeless after all. I was now full-time Jian Yang. I had to get in touch with my former fresh-off-the-boat self. I had to remember how to immigrant again. I listened to Chinese radio for an hour before every scene to get into Jian Yang's Chinese state of mind. And before the start of every take, I repeated a mantra in Mandarin, "我不知道 (Wo Bu Zhi Dao)," which means "I don't know." This summed up Jian Yang's entire being. He always has a general "I don't give a fuck" attitude. Either he doesn't want to deal with it, or he genuinely doesn't know what is going on.

The great thing about playing Jian Yang is that the worse I looked, the funnier it was. Our costume designer, Christina

Mongini, picked out a closetful of terrible-looking clothes for Jian Yang, and it was perfect. Jian Yang's wardrobe consisted of ugly sweaters and ill-fitting jeans; it looked like things from a suitcase he brought over from the old country. For the first time in my career, I actually had a wardrobe for my character, instead of just one outfit for the one day of work. This foster child had finally found a home. Jian Yang was here to stay.

My first scene as a series regular on *Silicon Valley* was the mansion party scene in season two, where Jian Yang and Erlich Bachman tried to get into the fancy Muir Woods charity party. Christina and I made sure Jian Yang had an ill-fitting tuxedo with a crooked clip-on bowtie. In between takes, a background actor came up and politely tried to fix my bowtie. "It's supposed to be like that," I said as I put it back to a forty-five-degree angle. Everything clicked in that scene. TJ and I were having so much fun, we forgot we were even acting. It was more like two friends messing with each other at a party. We discovered the clear and effective game of Erlich belittling Jian Yang only to have Jian Yang completely throw him under the bus. The dynamic of a big buffoon and the little troublemaker just worked.

There are four geniuses that are the creative motors behind *Silicon Valley*. The Four Amigos are made up of Mike Judge, Alec Berg, Clay Tarver and Dan O'Keefe. Mike's creations were the bloodline of modern American satire. He had created *Beavis and Butt-Head, King of the Hill, Office Space, Idiocracy*, and now *Silicon Valley*. The man is quietly one of the most genius comedic minds in all of entertainment. Alec and Dan were longtime *Seinfeld* writers; those two and Clay were all well-decorated Harvard graduate writers with a sharp sense of humor. These Four Amigos were responsible for writing the show and Mike and Alec were also the showrunners who directed most of the episodes. It's such a luxury to have these guys on set, sitting at video village. They would throw out alts (alternate lines, ideas) in between takes to give us more arsenal than just the original script. The great alts from the Four Amigos, mixed with the improvised lines from the actors, made each scene truly come alive.

During the mansion party scene, as Erlich tried to finagle his way into the fancy party, TJ improvised, "Ten minutes max, one cocktail or two, three max, he doesn't eat," pointing to Jian Yang. Alec Berg came over and threw me a line: "Say, 'Yes, I'm hungry.'" I did it on the next take and it worked perfectly. Then Jian Yang turned around and screamed out into the crowd, to Erlich's ultimate embarrassment, "Does anybody have an extra ticket, my investor cannot pay!" I went back to the receptionist. "Check again, please. E-R-I-C-A-R . . ." "That's not at all how it's spelled," the receptionist responded. I spelled the name in every possibly wrong way in each take. I decided to pronounce Erlich as Eric, not so much because of Jian Yang's accent but because Jian Yang doesn't care to pronounce his name correctly. And TJ tried every way to usher Jian Yang out of the party as fast as he could. In one take he wrestled me, in another take he just screamed, "Jian Yang!!!" which became one of his signature curses.

That night, Clay Tarver came up and told us Erlich and Jian Yang were like the modern-day Laurel and Hardy. As much as they might hate each other on the surface, there was a sense of comradery underneath, just like Laurel and Hardy. It was like familiarity breeds contempt, except it was more like contempt breeds familiarity. The underlying friendship was like a love story with a touch of Stockholm syndrome. That mansion scene has always been one of my favorite days on *Silicon Valley*. It will forever feel like the day Jian Yang and Erlich consummated.

The hardest part about working with TJ was keeping a straight face. I cracked up many times during a take. Our goal was to always make each other and the crew laugh. If we could hear laughter from video village, we knew we did something right. As a stand-up, it helped to pretend there was an audience. It became a little game where TJ and I tried to crack each other up during takes. TJ always won.

I once asked him:

"How do you not crack up in the middle of a scene? What's your secret?"

He jokingly responded, "I just don't find any of this funny. That's my secret."

I finally broke him with a little skim milk chalice.

Some of the best moments came alive in *Silicon Valley* because of Mike's and Alec's willingness to try things and play around with a scene. I learned to swing for the fences when it came to improvisation. That's the great thing about TV and film: you only need one take that works. You can go for the home run every time, and you only have to hit one. And the greatest thing a director can say to an actor is "Let's try it." In season four, when Erlich and Jian Yang went to their investor Lori Bream's baby shower, I found a tiny little skim milk chalice on the table next to the baby shower cake. I brought the tiny chalice over to Mike Judge and asked, "Can I try something with this?" Mike said, "Let's try it." On the next take, I entered the scene with the skim milk chalice and drank it in front of TJ. He finally broke and cracked up. In the next take, TJ brought the whole gag to life when he put his face in his hands in disbelief and said, "What are you drinking skim milk out of?" And I responded, "It's half half." Which is how my mom says half and half.

The prank calls from Jian Yang to Erlich became unexpected fan favorites.

> "Eric Bachman, is your refrigerator running? This is Mike Hunt."

To be honest, I had my doubts about the prank calls when I first read them in the script. But when they got a great reaction at the table read, I realized I should never doubt the Four Amigos. The prank calls perfectly painted Jian Yang's and Erlich's love-hate annoying brother relationship. And it also perfectly described Jian Yang's relationship with the English language. He had learned some canned jokes like "Is your refrigerator running?" and "Mike Hunt" from somewhere, but he just hadn't quite got the hang of how to use them. This was like when I was fifteen and I tried to put together a shitty combination of rap lyrics based on the raps I'd heard on BET.

"Eric Bachman, this is your mom, and you are not my baby."

"Eric Bachman, this is you as old man. I'm ugly and I'm dead, alone."

These prank calls became some of the most classic Jian Yang versus Erlich Bachman moments. I still get random Facebook messages from fans asking me to prank call their friends. Some have even offered me money, upwards of a whopping fifty bucks.

One night, I got an unexpected phone call from TJ in real life. It was midnight and I was already half asleep. I rolled over to my nightstand and picked up my phone.

"Hey, what's up, TJ?"

"Hey, Jimmy, you got a minute?"

"Sure."

This sounded serious; I was hoping he wasn't about to confess to a murder.

"You're the first one I'm calling about this." He takes a deep breath. "I'm not coming back next season."

Is TJ prank calling me in real life to get back at me for all the times I prank called him on the show? I surely hoped so.

"I'm quitting the show," TJ said.

This was for real. It felt like my best friend had just told me he was moving away to a different country. My heart sank. This meant Erlich's and Jian Yang's last scene on season four was our last scene ever.

TJ explained, "It was a hard decision, but I have to focus on my movie career. I have to take a chance."

"What about just coming back for a few episodes?" I knew his mind was already made up, but I'd regret it if I didn't ask him to stay.

"It's hard. It was a hard decision. But I'm doing it. You're the one I'm going to miss the most on the show."

"Thanks, TJ." I respected his decision as a friend and a colleague. There wouldn't have been a Jian Yang without Erlich.

This was me and TJ's very last take together on *Silicon Valley*. The end of the dynamic duo: Erlich and Jian Yang, Laurel and Hardy, Karl Malone and John Stockton.

If stand-up was my bachelor's degree in comedy, *Silicon Valley* was my PhD. I didn't just go to work; I went to school: Christopher Evan Welch's masterful table read, TJ's dazzling improvisations, the Four Amigos' brilliance, everyone's excellence in acting, costume design, camera work, props and everything else behind the scenes from the crew. It was the best education anyone could ever get in comedy. ~~I would pay to be on a show like this.~~ (My agent suggested I don't say this, so I can continue to get paid to be on the show.) *Silicon Valley* was my career-defining big break. And I was able to share my immigrant experiences through Jian Yang's character. From being a lost college graduate at Mike Judge's commencement speech to working with him on *Silicon Valley* was an American dream come true.

CHAPTER NINE

HOW TO HOLLYWOOD

I was suddenly thrown into a fantasy world. It was the HBO Golden Globes after-party at the Beverly Hilton. *Silicon Valley* had been nominated for Best Comedy Series and I was invited to the party along with my fellow castmates. The party was decked out in the *Game of Thrones* fire and ice theme with a massive HBO logo projected on the side of the Beverly Hilton. There was an open bar with top-shelf liquor, all the food a man could eat and all the who's who of Hollywood gathered inside of one swanky party.

My first stop was the posh buffet line; there were rib-eye steak and three different kinds of fish. This buffet was beyond Guam's wildest dreams. I was determined to stuff myself stupid to make up for all the times I ate at HomeTown Buffet. A man leaned in behind me to get a closer look at the salmon. I was about to tell him to back off my precious buffet fantasy, and then I turned around and realized it was Bryan Cranston. "Hey, just checking out what they have here," That caught me so off guard that I practically screamed at him and shoved my plate of salmon in his face. "The salmon looks good! You want some?" He kindly smiled at my mini mental breakdown and turned around to say hi to his friend. "Hey, Patrick!" I looked up; it was Sir Patrick Stewart. I looked over to the bar and I saw Mike Judge, so I moseyed over to say what's up. As I got closer, I saw that he was busy chatting with Marilyn Manson, and Dave Grohl from the Foo Fighters and Nirvana. So I back-peddled away with my overloaded plate of high-end meats. Then I saw Harrison Ford casually having a conversation with Jon Hamm, who was holding a shiny Golden Globe statue that he'd just won that night. I was so starstruck I almost rolled into a Short Round impression: "Watch out, Mister Jones!" I was hyperventilating. I walked towards the bathrooms for a breather, and there was Jennifer Aniston strolling out of the women's room. *Holy shit!* I stopped and stared at her as my brain kept telling me: *Don't stare, don't stare, don't stare.* But my body was frozen. I'm pretty sure I was experiencing a stroke at that moment. I felt like I was high on LSD, having the trip of a lifetime. *This can't be real life. Six months ago, I was driving drunk assholes in an Uber; now I am eating free salmon next to Harrison Ford?* My imposter syndrome kicked into full swing. I felt like I snuck into this party. *How did I end up here? I don't deserve this! These are gods amongst men and I am just a dude who used to pay five dollars to do five minutes at an open mic.* I was looking over my shoulder, waiting for a security guard to escort me out.

Being a series regular on a hit television show was beyond my wildest dreams. My very first acting coach, Caryn West, told us to write down the biggest goals we had and put them away in a box. Then we'd revisit it every six months to see if we could cross off any of these goals. With *Silicon Valley*, I was finally able to cross out a few of them.

~~Become a series regular on a TV show~~
~~Stop driving Uber~~
~~Get my own apartment~~

It felt great to accomplish something so unbelievable, but I didn't feel any different. I might be at the same buffet line as Bryan Cranston, but I still felt like the guy who was rejected by the agent at the apartment rental office. I was still the same guy with the same problems. My parents' attitudes hadn't changed. My friend asked my dad during dinner once:

"Isn't it great that Jimmy is on a TV show? He's doing so well."
"Yes, he's doing good. But I still wish he was a scientist," my dad unapologetically said right in front of my face.
"Why?" Jeremy pushed for more answers when I would have quit while I was just slightly behind.

"Scientist is always more respectable than an artist," my dad explained in a matter-of-fact way, as if that was the universal truth. I guess it is the truth in Chinese culture, which is the only universe he knows.

The first time I showed my mom a scene from *Silicon Valley*, she said:

"Jimmy, how many times do I have to tell you, don't hunch your back."

"Mom, this is acting, I'm playing a character."

"Can you play a character that stands up straight? You look weak." I gave up trying to explain myself. Nothing has changed.

I used to think being on TV meant I'd be living like the stars on MTV's *Cribs* in a mansion with three Ferraris, a pet tiger in the backyard and models lining up in front of my house waiting to date me. Nope. I still drive a Prius, I still use Tinder and I still dwell in a one-bedroom apartment, which is already a massive upgrade from living with Tarrell with Guam in my closet. I get recognized once in a while at the local bowling alley and I get a free beer if I'm lucky. Fans often come up to me and ask, "Are you Jian Yang?" I don't mind being called Jian Yang, but I have noticed there's always a hesitation when they ask me that question. Because if I wasn't the guy who played Jian Yang and I was just some random Asian guy, they would look super racist. I'm sure there were other Asians who were asked that question, and they had to respond, "Not all Asian people look alike, you asshole."

Then some people are shocked when they find out I sound nothing like Jian Yang:

"Oh my God, we love *Silicon Valley!* We didn't even know you speak English in real life. We thought that was your real accent!"

I bet nobody ever said to Johnny Depp, "We love *Pirates of the Caribbean*! We thought you were a pirate in real life!"

The majority of people who watch *Silicon Valley* are dudes. Ninety-five percent of girls who have come up to me always say:

"Oh my God! My boyfriend is a huge fan of *Silicon Valley!* Can I take a picture with you? It'll make him so happy!"
Sure, I'll make your boyfriend's day.

Meanwhile, I was still trying to find myself a girlfriend on Tinder. It's pretty awkward to be a quasi-celebrity on Tinder. Some girls don't believe it's really me. I mean, who the hell would use my picture as their fake profile picture? That's counterproductive. The girls who do believe it's me would always message me Jian Yang quotes from *Silicon Valley*. Most of their messages start with:

"I eat the fish!"

I used to think, *It's a clear sign that she's into me if she's a fan of the show.* I used to reply with some small talk like, "What's your favorite sushi restaurant?" Or another line from the show like, "What about garbage?" Yes, it was super lame. And I've since learned to not engage with someone who matched with me only because I'm on TV.

I once took this Tinder girl out to a dinner date. She was a very attractive girl from Orange County who had mentioned she was a big fan of *Silicon Vallcy.* My naïveté led me to believe that I was in for the win. We chitchatted about life and she asked me a few questions about working on *Silicon Valley.* She seemed like a sweet girl who was genuinely curious about my career. I swiped my credit card and threw down a 30 percent tip like I was a series regular on *Everybody Loves Raymond.* Then I smoothly asked her:

"Do you want to grab a drink after this?"

She said. "Let's go back to your place."

Wow, being on a TV show IS some kind of magical aphrodisiac.

When we hopped into my 2006 Prius, I felt like I needed to explain why I wasn't driving a Ferrari: "This thing gets like fifty miles a gallon." I wanted her to think that maybe I could totally afford a Ferrari but I chose to drive a Prius because I'm a hero who cares about the environment. I took the more roundabout scenic route in the neighborhood where we passed by fancy multimillion-dollar mansions before we finally arrived at my shabby apartment. The old metal garage gate at my apartment complex swung open and I turned the radio up to cover up the rusty creak. "I love this song!" I yelled over the newest Ariana Grande single. When we got to my place, I asked her:

"Do you want something to drink?"

And she said. "Let's go to your bedroom."

Holy shit! This being on TV thing is really fucking awesome!

She followed me into my room. Then she said:

"Can I look in your closet?"

Okay, maybe celebrities are supposed to have sex in the closet, I'm down to try something new.

So I showed her to my closet. It was filled with unimpressive clothes from Ross, but at least there wasn't a dude named Guam sleeping in there. She didn't say a word and started to shuffle through the clothes. I wasn't sure where this was going anymore. So I joked:

"Are you looking for a new outfit?"

She turned around and we locked eyes. This was my moment. I leaned in for the kiss. And she pushed me away like Emmitt Smith viciously stiff-arming a linebacker.

"Woah! I think you got the wrong idea," she said.

Wrong idea?! You invited yourself back to my place. Then into my bedroom! What idea was I supposed to have?!

I was completely stumped. Then she said:

"I just wanted to see how you lived and what you have in your closet. But maybe I should go."

What is that supposed to mean? See how I lived and what I have in my closet? What kind of sick shit is that? What is this, an episode of MTV Cribs?!

I was beyond confused. I guess she literally just wanted to see what I had in my closet? Maybe she was an aspiring costume designer? Maybe my car and apartment weren't baller enough for her? Or maybe she was just a crazy person. She left and I never went out with a *Silicon Valley* fan from Tinder again.

Like most people in this world, I thought achieving my goals would solve all my life's problems. It didn't change much at all. There's satisfaction in achievement, but the excitement is in the chase. Looking back, some of the happiest times of my life were working at the Comedy Palace for minimum wage, folding envelopes with Tarrell and Guam. Even though none of us had any money, we had a great time just hanging out. I was so poor I would go into the kitchen and sneak out leftover prime rib with a side of beef barley soup. Once a fortnight, the comedians went to Denny's after the shows; that was our special treat. I had to save up to get a ten-dollar Moons Over My Hammy at Denny's, but that ham sandwich meant something to me. I earned it by doing what I loved and it tasted just as good as the salmon at the Golden Globes party. One night after the Comedy Palace shows, Tarrell, Guam, our comedian friend Jason Lawhead and I were chopping it up over a grand slam breakfast at two in the morning.

I said to my boys, "I think the new waitress likes me, she was giving me some signals. She—"

"Jimmy," Jason interrupted, "her boyfriend drives a Bentley, you were stealing soup in the kitchen." We all folded over laughing.

We are so busy chasing our goals, sometimes we forget about the thrill of the chase. We only realize the goal wasn't the prize when we get there. It was cool to be in the same room with Sir

Pat Stew and Jen Ann, but I honestly had more fun at Denny's than the Golden Globes party. Maybe Charles Dickens and UCSD chancellor Fox did have a point after all: "It was the best of times, it was the worst of times, it was the age of wisdom, it was the age of foolishness."

I had achieved one of my biggest goals when I became a series regular on *Silicon Valley*, but I felt more lost than ever. *Now what?* I was meandering around in my apartment not knowing what to do next with my life. I panicked. It was scary to feel empty in the presence of success. So I called my mentor, Sean Kelly, as I always do when I'm lost. I asked Sean, "What should I do now?" And he said: "Start back at square one, with an even crazier goal." Then I realized, the chase is never over. I just needed new challenges. It's satisfying to cross out a goal, but it's even more exciting to write down new ones. So I wrote down some even crazier goals:

~~Become a series regular on a TV show~~
~~Stop driving Uber~~
~~Get my own apartment~~
Win an Oscar
Meet Snoop Dogg

HOW TO ASIAN IN HOLLYWOOD

I auditioned for another immigrant role that couldn't have been more different from Jian Yang. It was for *Patriots Day*, a dramatic feature recounting the 2013 Boston Marathon bombing, directed by Peter Berg, starring Mark Wahlberg, Kevin Bacon, John

Goodman, J. K. Simmons and Michelle Monaghan. The cast of this film was more impressive than the Last Supper's. The role was a based-on-real-life-character named Dun Meng. Dun, or as he liked to be called, Danny, was a Chinese immigrant just like me. He had just moved from China to Boston when he was carjacked at gunpoint and kidnapped by the terrorists after the Boston Marathon bombing. Danny's heroic escape played a key role in the capture of the two terrorist brothers. He was a real American hero. Playing him would be an honor. It would also be my first dramatic role in a feature film. This was the new challenge that I had been looking for.

Every article I read about Danny Meng, I became more in awe of his heroism. He was held up at gunpoint and they loaded explosives into the back of his car. The terrorists drove Danny around for a nerve-wrecking ninety minutes. They were on their way to Times Square in New York for another bombing. When they pulled over at a gas station, Danny took a chance and made a heroic escape. He sprinted out of the car, nearly escaping the grasp of one of the terrorists. Then he made the 911 call that helped law enforcement track down the vehicle, which led to the shootout in Watertown and the eventual apprehension of the two heinous terrorists. I found the incredible surveillance footage of Danny sprinting away from the terrorists, and the chilling recording of the 911 call from Danny. It was terrifying and intense. I tried to put myself in Danny's shoes that night, and I am not sure if I'd have the courage and presence of mind to do what he did. Danny Meng is a hero.

I auditioned for the prolific casting director Sheila Jaffe twice before auditioning in front of the director, Peter Berg. Pete and

I started off casually chatting about stand-up comedy, and then Pete just rolled into the scene. He pretended to carjack me like the terrorists did to Danny. I was ready. I sprinted out of the imaginary car and hid behind the imaginary gas station cashier like I'd seen in the real-life surveillance video. Then I made the 911 phone call just like I'd heard on the actual recorded version. Pete was acting with me every step of the way; we were in the moment. At the end of the audition, I felt an ounce of what Danny went through that night. And it was terrifying. Pete asked me:

"So how do you feel about cutting your hair for this role?"

"Yeah, I'd definitely cut my hair for this role."

"I didn't ask you if you would cut your hair, I asked you how do you feel about cutting your hair."

I got the part.

I was nervous about how I'd be received as a dramatic actor, but I was more nervous about how Danny Meng would receive me as an actor playing him in a movie. We had to "get it right." That was the mantra on set. The movie wasn't about us; it was about honoring the victims and heroes of this event. And my role was to tell the real story of Danny Meng, an average guy who became a hero in desperate times. I made sure his accent was genuine, the story was accurate and his emotions were real.

Danny was a Chinese immigrant from the Sichuan province. He had a Chinese accent but it was different than Jian Yang's. He had a very specific Sichuan accent where he pronounces *n*'s in place of *l*'s. Instead of saying "lonely" he'd say it like "noneny."

I worked on that accent every day for at least four hours for the month leading up to filming. I went to the grocery store, the post office and the mechanic speaking in that accent. What I learned was more than the accent itself. I noticed how crudely people treated a foreigner. The mechanic was quickly annoyed because he could barely understand me, the cashier at the grocery store avoided eye contact and the post office lady couldn't be more frustrated trying to explain the difference between priority and first-class mail to me. This reminded me of my own struggles when I first came to this country. I looked up to Danny as a hero, and I empathized with Danny as a fellow immigrant.

In one of the opening scenes of the film, Danny facetimes his parents back in China and they speak Mandarin to each other. They had cast a father who spoke Mandarin with a heavy Cantonese accent. The American audience might not notice the difference, but to a Chinese speaker that's like someone playing a British character with a southern drawl. To me, that was unacceptable. We had to "get it right." So I went up to Pete and voiced my concerns. Pete agreed. "Let's find you a new dad." A light bulb went off in my head. "Why don't we just hire my real dad, he's an actor." Pete trusted my word as an actor and appreciated my sentiment as a son. They flew my real dad out to Boston the following week and he played my movie dad in *Patriots Day*. That scene is the best father-and-son memento we can ever have in our family.

The entire film shot in Boston. We stayed in a hotel that eerily overlooked the finish line of the Boston Marathon, the same place where the bombs went off in 2013. I was able to get in touch with Danny, who still lived across the river in Cambridge. We hit it off right away. We spoke Mandarin to each other and shared our Chinese immigrant experiences. He created and managed a start-up food delivery app called RushRunner that specialized in delivering the most authentic Chinese foods in Boston. His real life wasn't too far off from my pretend life on *Silicon Valley*. Danny told me, "I've seen you on *2 Broke Girls*." Apparently *2 Broke Girls* was one of the most popular American shows in China, and my two lines on that show were my first introduction to Danny. He was so open to sharing everything with me. We sat down at Danny's shared-space office as he recounted the fateful night to me. I had a good sense of what happened that night through my research; I wanted to find out what Danny was thinking during that horrifying night. Danny said:

"I thought about my family, my friends and how I was never going to see them again."

That hit me. *What would I do if I thought I'd never see my family and friends ever again?* I felt honored that Danny would share these emotional details with me. Then he told me one detail that deeply affected me:

"When the terrorist jumped into the car and pointed his gun at me, he asked me, 'Is there anyone who cared about you here?' And I said, 'No.'"

"Why did you say no?" I asked. "Didn't you want to plead for his empathy?"

"No, he wasn't asking me because he cared. He was asking me to see if there will be anyone who'll call the police if I'm gone. So I said no, nobody care about me here."

Each answer he gave to the terrorists that night could mean life or death. Even with a gun pointed to his head, Danny kept his smarts and composure.

Danny continued, "And really, that was the truth. Nobody really cared about me here. I was new to America, most of my friends were in China."

That gave me the chills. Every immigrant has felt that way: "Nobody cares about me here." I know I definitely felt that way when I first came to America. I might not have been able to relate to being carjacked at gunpoint by terrorists, but I could surely relate to the loneliness of being an immigrant.

I took that part of the story to Peter Berg the next morning. "We have to put that in the movie," I said. Pete, being one of the best directors I've ever worked with, said, "Let's try it." He was the ultimate actor's director. He started his career as an actor and he understood how actors work. He didn't give us any technical notes and he just let us play out the scenes. There were no marks and he never said to open up to camera; he let us stay in the moment and play it real.

I was nervous about filming the carjacking scene; it was a tough experience to re-create what happened that night in the car and I needed to do right by Danny. With Pete's directing style and the great actors Themo Melikidze and Alex Wolff who portrayed the terrorist brothers, everything felt so real. I completely broke down during one take. I thought about my own family and how I'd never see them again. Those weren't tears that I learned to conjure from acting classes; they were real. The scene felt so real that I had nightmares for a week after the shoot. I would wake up in the middle of the night and think someone was standing on the foot of my bed. I could only imagine what Danny had gone through after the real carjacking.

Patriots Day wasn't nominated for any awards, but it was the proudest thing that I'd ever done in my career, to portray a Chinese immigrant hero in such a quintessential American story. Everyone who knows Danny's story thinks he's a hero, except for Danny. Danny said, "I don't think I'm a hero. A hero is somebody who is willing to sacrifice himself to save somebody else. I was just trying to save myself that night." To me, his humbleness makes him even more of a hero. Danny makes me proud to be an immigrant.

Danny called me after he saw an early screening of the movie. "You were very good." That meant more to me than winning any award.

I take pride in playing immigrant characters. I've come across people who had a negative opinion about playing Asian characters that have an accent. I've even met Asian actors who won't audition for a role that has an Asian accent. They believe these accented characters reinforce the stereotype of an Asian being the constant foreigner. Frankly, I can't relate. I was an immigrant. And no matter how Americanized I become, no matter how much Jay-Z I listen to, I'll always be an immigrant. Just because I don't speak English with an accent anymore doesn't mean that I'm better than the people who do. My job as an actor is not to judge anyone and portray a character with humanity. There are real people with real Asian accents in the real world. I used to be one of them. And I'm damn proud of it.

To me, the issue is not the people who speak with an Asian accent; it's the perception of the accent itself. Sofía Vergara's

Mark Wahlberg, me and Danny Meng. Two Chinese immigrants, three Americans.

Spanish accent is considered sexy, and it helped her become an international sex symbol. Peter Sellers's Inspector Clouseau French accent in the Pink Panther movies was praised in the comedy world, and it earned him a Golden Globe nomination for best actor. But why is the Chinese accent considered foreign and nerdy? Jian Yang is more than a fresh-off-the-boat immigrant; he's also a funny, devious little asshole. Danny Meng is not just a foreign Chinese student; he's a real-life American hero who helped capture the Boston Marathon bombing terrorists. I want people to see these guys and say, "Wow, that Chinese dude is awesome." And I want girls to watch these roles and say, "I need to find myself a Jian Yang or Danny Meng. These guys are fucking sexy." My mission is not to avoid playing an immigrant; my mission is to make Asian immigrants as sexy as Ryan Gosling.

HOW TO BE SEXY

My sexiness was finally noticed when I was cast in the film *Life of the Party.* It's a Melissa McCarthy–Ben Falcone comedy about a mom who goes back to college and joins her daughter's sorority. The description for my character is "Maddie's perfect boyfriend." And as this small world would have it, Molly Gordon, who played my girlfriend Maddie in the film, is the daughter of Bryan Gordon, the director who wanted to cast me for *Sin City Saints,* which led me to being a series regular on *Silicon Valley.* Playing a boyfriend might not seem like a big deal, but playing a white girl's boyfriend is like the Holy Grail for Asian actors. It has always been rare for an Asian male to go out with a white female in mainstream media. Jackie Chan never had a white girl; Bruce Lee married a white girl in real life but he never had a white girl in the movies. But on the flip side, Lucy Liu had plenty of white beaus. It's a self-fulfilling prophecy; we don't see a lot of Asian men with white women on-screen, so we don't risk putting a lot of Asian men with white women on-screen. I was happy to help change that.

I was actually a bit uncomfortable being the "perfect boyfriend." I was used to being a funny character actor on-screen and I have never been the perfect boyfriend in real life. My whole life, I've always felt like I had to be funny to compensate for my lack of aesthetics. I felt insecure about playing the straight-man boyfriend. *What do I bring to the table? Looks? Charm? How could I be the perfect boyfriend when I couldn't even navigate through a Tinder date?* I could hear my dad saying, "You? Ha-ha-ha-ha, come on."

Melissa and Ben believed that I could be the perfect boyfriend before I ever did. They never thought for a second that it was unusual to have an Asian boyfriend and a white girl on the big screen. They saw me beyond my ethnicity. I had to put my insecurity aside and put the Asian nation on my back. This was not just about me; this was about making all my Asian brothers look sexy. So I decided to do some research on how to be sexy.

The movie shot in Atlanta. On a Saturday night, I went out to a dance club by myself, for research for the role, obviously. I'm not usually a dance club type of guy, but when in Atlanta, I was supposed to be sexy. The club was a cool underground spot playing the latest dirty south hip-hop joints. I threw back a couple drinks, and I was ready to cut a rug. Then a cute girl approached me and asked, "Do you want some Molly?" I'm usually not a Molly type of guy, but when in Atlanta, I was supposed to be sexy. So she dabbed her finger in a small plastic bag of white powder and stuffed that finger right into my mouth. I'd never done Molly before. Ten minutes later, everything felt like Disneyland. I was in love with everything and everyone. I had the confidence to go up to every girl in the club; I finally felt sexy. I'm sure in reality, I was probably dancing like somebody's drunk aunt at a quinceañera. Three hours later, I was still feeling great, the club was closing but I wanted to keep dancing. Six hours later, I was still ready to party but everything was already closed. Twelve hours later, I was pacing around in my hotel room with my heart beating out of my chest. My body was dead tired but my mind was wide awake. I drank a couple glasses of red wine and I took some NyQuil, to no avail. The next thing I knew, I hadn't slept for forty hours and I was on the brink of cardiac arrest. That definitely wasn't just Molly; pretty sure that finger was laced with meth. I had to be back on set in eight hours. I lay on my bed with my eyes wide open.

I didn't sleep a wink that weekend and got on set with massive dark circles under my eyes. My eye bags felt like grocery bags and my face looked like a panda. I'm pretty sure I aged five years in two days. I pretended to be the perfect boyfriend while my body was about to shut down from methamphetamine. I somehow managed to power through the scenes without collapsing. Luckily, the scene was an eighties-themed party scene, so everyone looked ridiculous anyway. Maybe this was method acting for this party boy, or more precisely, meth acting. I survived that day and practically went into a coma and slept for twenty hours. Nobody ever found out this perfect boyfriend was doing meth on the weekend, until now. Little did they know Jimmy was far from a perfect boyfriend; he was a dipshit who let random girls stick drugs in his mouth.

FRESH TO DEF

I got a call from my manager one afternoon. "Hey, you want to go to the All Def Movie Awards?" The All Def Movie Awards was like the urban Oscars. It was an award show created by Russell Simmons to champion diversity in film. So of course I went. The next thing I knew, I was in the same building as Snoop Dogg, Ice Cube, LL Cool J. I looked at the name tags at my table—Tommy Davidson, Mark Curry, Too Short—two of the best comedians and one of the most legendary rappers that I grew up watching on BET. There was an award that night called "Best Performance by an Asian Not Asked to Use an Accent." I'm not making this up. I was invited to attend the show because I was nominated for that award for my role in *Patriots Day*, in which I did have an accent. The other nominees were Randall Park and, also, Donnie Yen from *Star Wars* who naturally had a Chinese accent. The award was supposed to be ironic, really; it should have been called "Best Asian Homie Award." And as if it was a dream come true, I won. It was the pinnacle of being an Asian actor who grew up watching BET. This was the very first award I'd ever won for my acting and it couldn't have been more fitting to receive it in front of everyone who taught me English. This was my Oscar.

I jumped onstage to receive my golden All Def statue; it looked like an Oscar except the dude on the statue was the dude from *Super Fly*. I gave a speech in front of all of my heroes:

"Wow, an Asian winning an award on the All Def show, this is a dream come true."

I looked over to Russell Simmons:

"Thank you, Russ. You have no idea who I am but that's okay . . . This is big, man, I guess I'm doing it on behalf of Jackie Chan, Yao Ming, Lucy Liu." The crowd laughed. "This is about diversity. I was an immigrant, I was the dude with an accent and I learned to speak English by watching BET *Rap City* with Snoop, Cube, LL Cool J and *Def Comedy Jam*, so all my heroes are here. Thank you, guys, very much." I pointed to my heroes in the audience, and I saw Snoop Dogg clapping through a cloud of weed smoke surrounding him. Then I pointed to Snoop Dogg's mentor in the audience, the infamous pimp who is always dressed in green and gold, and I signed off with one of his signature pimp catchphrases. "Thank you, Don 'Magic' Juan, you're my hero. Green for the money, gold for the honey."

When I got off the stage, I walked through a thick cloud of weed smoke and saw Snoop Dogg. Snoop gave me the coolest handshake and said, "Good job, homie." This was the crowning moment of my career.

~~Become a series regular on a TV show~~
~~Stop driving Uber~~
~~Get my own apartment~~
~~Win an Oscar~~
~~Meet Snoop Dogg~~

I was invited to do a podcast at Too Short's studio the next week and I got to hang out with the legend himself. Too Short is a West Coast rapper whose career spans from the eighties with hit singles such as "Gettin' It," "I'm a Player" and "The World Is Filled . . ." from Biggie's *Life After Death* album, to more recently, the Bay Area hit song "Blow the Whistle," where he famously says, "What's my favorite word? Bitch!" He is known as the man who made the word *bitch* famous in rap songs. His studio is a giant warehouse converted into three recording studios, a live sound stage, a room filled with arcade games and full living quarters. It was every artist's dream to be in that place.

On the podcast, we talked about BET, strip clubs and weed. For a kid that grew up in Hong Kong, I had a lot of common interests with a rapper who grew up in Oakland. I took a hit off of Too Short's blunt and I coughed for the next five minutes. He laughed and said, "You can't handle that Too Short weed." And he was right: one hit and I was high for the next eight hours. I confessed to Short during the podcast: "I actually used to make beats before I got into comedy," and I showed him some of my beats. He started bobbing his head. "This is good." That was the ultimate stamp of approval in hip-hop. All the days spent making beats for the Yellow Panthers had finally paid off.

In the Boombox studio with DJ Bobby Loco, Too Short and my golden All Def movie award. I was so high that I have no recollection of taking this picture.

I thought selling beats to Fudgestick.com was the pinnacle of my music career; now I found a new frontier collaborating with Too Short. Short rapped on one of my songs and I was featured in one of his music videos. It was one of my lifelong dreams come true. Stand-up and acting are my bread and butter, but there is always a special place in my heart for hip-hop music. When we shot the music video for the song called "You Came to Party," I knew exactly how to make it rain in that party bus from the hours of research I did on BET *Rap City*. The song also happened to be one of the end credit songs on *Silicon Valley* in season four. Jian Yang and Too Short made for a new dynamic duo.

This time, instead of asking myself, *Now what?* I had learned to enjoy the Now. Looking back to see how far I'd come from making music at Chris's apartment to making music in Too Short's studio gave me a brand new perspective. It's exciting to chase after a new goal, but it's meaningless if you can't sit down and enjoy the moment.

LIFE IS LIKE BUYING A FLAT-SCREEN TV

The day you buy your 55-inch flat screen and throw away your old Zenith tube TV is one of the best days of your life. You call all your buddies over and you watch *Planet Earth* for eight hours. It's magnificent. That flat screen marks a milestone for your success. You've made it. Then two months later, you get used to the 55-inch TV; it's just another TV to you. You watch the *Price Is Right* on it and scream, "One dollar! Bid one dollar, you fucking idiot!" just like you did when you had your Zenith tube TV. And sadly, you can't go back to your Zenith tube TV. You have tricked your brain into a new standard and there's nowhere to go but up. So you set a new goal to buy the newest 75-inch 4K TV. You save an extra hundred dollars every paycheck, and it feels exciting. You visualize the awesomeness of 4K in your dreams every day. You finally go to Best Buy and pick up your new baby. It's the happiest day of your life, and the picture is better than your eyeballs can handle.

You invite all your buddies over and you watch *Monday Night Football* in majestic 4K. You can even see a piece of Tom Brady's perfect brown hair flow in the wind as he delivers the perfect spiral. It's so awesome you get hard a little bit. Then another two months later, you're sitting there alone screaming at Brady because you are coming up short in your Fantasy Football League. "Throw another touchdown, you fucking asshole!" And now the 75-inch TV becomes the new normal, yet again. Your amazing TV becomes just another TV. You can't even go watch the games at Buffalo Wild Wings with your boys anymore because their 65-inch TV now looks like a Zenith tube TV to you. You go back to watching the *Price Is Right*, verbally abusing the contestants. Everything is still the same as when you had the Zenith tube TV. Then they roll out a new OLED super-high-def 85-inch TV. You're motivated again, striving to get the new standard. But now you understand the cycle. You look back and see how far you've come from the crappy Zenith, and it gives you a whole new appreciation for the 75-inch TV you have in front of you. You learn to enjoy *Monday Night Football* again while you remain excited for the OLED 85-inch TV in your future.

CHAPTER TEN

HOW TO AMERICAN

I finally became a US citizen in 2015. I had been qualified to become a US citizen for several years, but it cost $725 to file the paperwork. I wasn't unpatriotic; I just didn't have $725 to spare until 2015. The main differences between a US permanent resident with a green card and a US citizen are the right to vote, the right to sit on a hung jury and the right to not get deported if you claim you're a US citizen at the Tijuana border. I was finally convinced that I needed to become a US citizen when a friend told me his buddy with a green card was deported after he was charged with domestic abuse. I wasn't planning on beating my imaginary wife, but I realized I could have gotten deported for something trivially illegal like smoking weed in public. That wasn't a chance I was willing to take. Just to be clear: domestic violence is terrible and all perpetrators should be deported to an island where they beat each other in a giant octagon, like a Thunderdome for assholes. All the logical factors aside, truthfully, I did feel a great sense of pride in finally becoming an American citizen.

To become a US citizen, I had to pass the civics test to prove that I had a good enough understanding of American history and the English language. I had to prepare for a Q&A from a booklet, "100 Civics Questions."

How many justices are on the Supreme Court?
What is the economic system of the United States?
What does the judicial branch do?

I have seen enough of the "Jaywalking" segment on *The Tonight Show with Jay Leno* to know that most US-born citizens wouldn't know the answers to these questions. I had to study those questions like it was the SATs. They should have let me pass the test just based on the amount of Bud Light and American football I'd consumed over the last ten years. I think the test should have more relevant everyday American questions like:

What constitutes pass interference in the NFL?
What's Snoop Dogg's real name?
Who is Leonardo DiCaprio currently dating?

The NFL, Snoop and Leo are just as quintessentially American as the Supreme Court.

The test took place in a stuffy room inside of an old brick building in downtown Los Angeles. I don't know why all government facilities have to look as dreadfully boring as possible. To properly welcome these potential new American citizens, the test should have taken place at a strip club. Leave a good impression and show everyone what America really has to offer. After an hour of sitting on the most uncomfortable government-issued plastic chair, they finally called my name: "Man . . . Shing . . . Ouuuuu . . . Yang?" It was exactly the same as my first day in school in America. "You can just call me Jimmy." The lady who interviewed me was a woman with a thick Jamaican accent. I am pretty sure that I was more Americanized than my American-citizenship interviewer. I bet you she didn't even know what constitutes pass interference in the NFL. I answered every question correctly like I was Ken Jennings on *Jeopardy*. After acing that test, I thought I'd get to meet the president and he'd congratulate me on my new citizenship. Instead, I had to wait another several months to become a US citizen at the naturalization ceremony. All I could think of during that time was, *Don't get arrested for smoking weed in public.*

I was one of three thousand people from eighty different countries at the Los Angeles Convention Center for the naturalization ceremony. It was a magical moment for everyone. I was surrounded by soon-to-be US citizens of every color, race and religion. Sitting next to me was a Mexican couple in their sixties, behind me was a Persian dude who looked like a classmate from

Beverly Hills High School and in front of me was an old Chinese couple who reminded me of my grandparents. It was truly a beautiful sight. People were crying from jubilation. Whatever journey they went through to become American citizens finally culminated in this moment that they shared with other fellow immigrants from all over the world. For me, it was especially sentimental because it meant I had $725 in my checking account. We sat down as a local politician took to the podium and congratulated us on this monumental day. Then they played a song accompanied by a music video on the big projector screen to welcome the three thousand newest citizens to the US of A. The video started with the classic eagle flying by, followed by beautiful farmland and a slow zoom-in shot of Mount Rushmore. Then the song came on.

"I'm proud to be an American where at least I know I'm free . . ."

The Mexican couple next to me put their hands on their chests as if it was the national anthem. I didn't have the heart to tell them this wasn't the "Star Spangled Banner"; it was Lee Greenwood's "God Bless the USA."

Everyone around me started to tear up, but I was too distracted by the crappy music video to be fully in touch with my emotions. *Really, America? This is the best music video we have?* Any music video from BET would be better than an eagle flying over an empty cornfield. Instead of Lee Greenwood's "God Bless the USA," I suggest we play Jay-Z's *Big Pimpin'* at the naturalization ceremony. Instead of flying eagles and Mount Rushmore, it should be partying on a yacht, popping Cristal with bikini models. We should show the newly anointed American citizens what it truly means to live the American dream:

"We doin' big pimpin' up in N.Y.C. It's just that jigga man, Pimp C, and B-U-N-B."

I would have cried if they played that. God bless America.

Everyone congratulated me for becoming an American citizen. But I didn't feel any different. I was still Asian. I was now officially an American person with an American passport, but I still looked like the same Asian kid who didn't know the Pledge of Allegiance. Nobody in any part of the world is going to come up to me and say, "Hey, American guy! Cool passport! Rocky Balboa!" No, random people still look at me and holler, "Hey, Karate Kid!" "Jackie Chan!" "Bruce Lee!" The color of my passport doesn't matter; most people will always see me as Asian before they'll think I'm American. It's hard to put ethnicities aside in the melting pot of America. Sometimes I identify so much with my ethnic background that I forget what I'm really about as a person.

I went to Winnipeg, Canada, for my first trip as an American citizen with my freshly minted US passport. It was for a weekend stand-up stint at the Rumor's Comedy Club, opening up for Shawn Wayans from *The Wayans Bros*. I got off the plane and strutted through the border security with my beautiful blue passport. *Finally, I'm an American that can't be told to go back to where I came from by the border patrol.* I laid my passport down in front of the Canadian border patrol officer like it was a badge of honor. She gave me a warm Canadian smile, probably impressed by how

American I was. Then she flipped through the empty pages and looked at my name. It's now Manshing Jimmy Ouyang; Jimmy is finally my official American middle name, not just a nickname. She looked up and asked, "So are you here for business or pleasure?" When I was young, I was taught by my parents to always say pleasure at border security for our family vacations. So I automatically replied, "Pleasure." And I gave her a confident American grin. She asked:

"So what brought you here to Winnipeg?" Now I had to back up my pleasure story, but it's okay. I'm a professional actor, I got this.

"Just to get away from LA, you know, all the craziness and traffic. I thought it'd be nice to go to somewhere quiet, and have a little vacation in Winnipeg." Nailed it, Tom Hanks.

"So you're not here to visit family or anything?"

"I mean I have a friend in town that I'm planning to see."

"What's his name?"

"Shawn . . . Warner."

"Sir, why don't you come with me."

Fuck.

She led me to a back room where, once again, there was a man holding an assault rifle. I was once again detained at the border. It was like déjà vu. It doesn't matter which citizenship I possess, I should generally stop lying at any country's border. She whispered something to the Teflon-vested man and she took a seat across from me. Her Canadian smile was gone. She said:

"Why don't you tell me the truth?"

You know when your mom catches you in an obvious lie, but you still try to stand your ground because you don't want to get caught lying? This was exactly that, except Mom doesn't have an armed guard behind her.

"I was telling the truth ma'am. I'm here to get away for a little vacation. Here to have fun."

"Nobody comes to Winnipeg to have fun," she said bluntly.

I couldn't argue with that. I guess I underestimated just how shitty Winnipeg was. I didn't know what to say. She typed something into the computer.

"Are you a stand-up comedian?"

"Umm . . ." *How did she know that?*

"Are you opening for Shawn Wayans this weekend?"

What the fuck? Is she psychic?

"Umm . . . No . . ." I resisted with one last lie.

She turned the computer screen around and showed me.

"Then why does it say on your Facebook page, 'I'm going to be in Winnipeg, Canada, this week—Rumor's Comedy Club! Opening for Shawn Wayans. Get your tickets now!'"

That was the most embarrassing moment of my life. I wished the guard would shoot me with the assault rifle to put me out of my misery. I put my hands over my face, not sure if I should cry or laugh at my own stupidity. She pressed on:

"Why did you feel like you had to lie?"

The jig was up, now I had to beg for mercy. "I am so sorry, I'm just a stupid person. I have no idea why I lied. I've never been on a business trip before. I'm so sorry."

She shook her head at this pathetic liar, and then she looked over to the armed guard. "What should we do with him?"

The guard said, "It's up to you. You can let him stay, or send him back to where he came from."

The same words the Tijuana border patrol said to me ten years ago haunted me again. But then I realized, this time "send him back to where he came from" meant sending me back to America, not Hong Kong. As twisted as it may sound, I felt pretty good about that sentence. Even though I was a stupid liar, for the first time in my life somebody actually saw me as an American citizen, not a Chinese immigrant. On the brink of getting deported from Canada, I felt more American than ever. America is now "where I came from." *I made it! I'm an American!*

She decided to have mercy on me and let me through to Winnipeg, where I performed nine sold-out shows with Shawn Wayans. Who said nobody comes to Winnipeg to have fun? Winnipeg was a blast for this American.

HOW TO HONG KONG

I hadn't been back to Hong Kong in seventeen years. A part of me had always avoided going back to the motherland. I was nervous it would ruin the perfect childhood I remembered; I didn't want to risk changing the perception of the positive memories I had from Hong Kong. *What if Hong Kong is nothing like I remember?*

I finally had an undeniable excuse to go back to Hong Kong when I landed a role in the *Crazy Rich Asians* movie filming in Singapore. *Crazy Rich Asians* is based on the *New York Times* bestselling book of the same name, written by Kevin Kwan. It takes us into a semi-fictional world of the ridiculously fabulous lifestyles and first-world problems of the filthy rich billionaire families living in Singapore. Kevin wanted to "introduce a contemporary

Asian to the North American audience." When the movie was announced, it made waves in the Asian community. *Crazy Rich Asians* would mark the first American major studio movie in twenty-five years to feature a full Asian cast since *The Joy Luck Club*. The actors, the producers and the director, Jon Chu, all shared the same sense of pride and responsibility to properly represent Asians in mainstream media with this monumental opportunity. This was our chance to show the world that we are just as brilliant, just as good looking and just as funny as everyone else in Hollywood. This was our key to open the doors for all the amazing Asian talents in cinema.

The most talented, most beautiful and funniest Asian actors from every corner of the world came together for this movie. There were no egos or superstars on the set. We all understood that we were making something much bigger than ourselves. We had Chinese legend Michelle Yeoh; Chinese American actors Constance Wu, Harry Shum Jr., Nora Lum and myself; Korean American comedy superstar Ken Jeong; Filipino American comedian Nico Santos; Chinese British actress Gemma Chan; Japanese British actress Sonoya Mizuno; Chinese Australian actors Chris Pang, Ronny Chieng, Remy Hii; British Malaysian leading man Henry Golding; and local Singaporean A-listers Fiona Xie and Pierre Png. It was my first time working with all of these amazing talents, but there was an immediate familiarity among all of us. Even though we were brought up in different countries, where some of us were immigrants and some of us were second and third generation, we shared the same experience of growing up Asian. We had all experienced being seen as Asian before being seen as American, British or Australian. We all shared the same experience of calling every older family friend "Uncle" and "Auntie." And we all grew up think-ing it was a farfetched idea to become an actor. It was an incredible feeling to be among these amazingly talented Asian brothers and sisters who understood each other. Everyone made each other feel even more proud to be Asian. For once in my life, I wanted to flaunt my Asian side instead of hiding it to fit in as somebody else.

Ever since I immigrated to America, I tried my hardest to be American. I made it a point to make friends from every ethnic background, instead of just Asian friends. I fought so hard to not be grouped in with the other Asians in college. I didn't want to be the Chinese kid who only hung out with other Chinese kids; I thought that was so lame and stereotypical. But after the *Crazy Rich Asians* shoot, I finally got it. It wasn't about choosing to hang out with people of the same skin tone; it was about hanging out with people who shared the same point of view because they had gone through the same experiences. One of my favorite lines in the *Crazy Rich Asians* script was "I didn't have to explain myself that I'm Asian here, I'm just another person." During the *Crazy Rich Asians* shoot in Singapore, everyone saw me as who I am. I wasn't just the Asian kid; I could just be the funny guy, instead of the Asian guy who is funny. I felt a weight lifted off my shoulders. It was the first time in seventeen years that I didn't have to prove to anyone, or myself, that I was more than the token Asian guy.

Crazy Rich Asians made me want to get in touch with my roots instead of running away from them. I flew to Hong Kong after we wrapped filming in Singapore. I went back to the motherland with a newly found sense of pride in my culture and myself. It had been so long that I got the same culture shock when I ar-rived in Hong Kong as I did the first day I arrived in Los Angeles.

Some of the crazy beautiful supporting cast of *Crazy Rich Asians*. LEFT TO RIGHT: Jing Lusi, Chris Pang, Gemma Chan, me, Harry Shum Jr., Fiona Xie, Sonoya Mizuno, Nico Santos, Carmen Soo, Remy Hii, Victoria Loke, Constance Lau, Ronny Chieng. Who wouldn't want to be Asian?

Instead of eight-lane boulevards filled with cars and strip malls, the streets in Hong Kong were packed with a sea of people and shops in a concrete jungle. The alleyways told the history of Hong Kong, with classic BBQ ducks hanging from the restaurant windows, century-old flea markets selling household items and mysterious fortune tellers preaching to the superstitious. I was captivated by the image of an old man wearing a wifebeater pushing an old wooden dolly in front of an ultramodern fifty-story glass building. The old Chinese culture blends perfectly with the new Westernized world. The city felt alive. In LA, I can walk for fifteen minutes and not see a single soul in a land of strip malls. In Hong Kong, you can't help but bump shoulders with the hundreds of people crossing the streets with purpose. There's an adventure in every corner of this controlled chaos. Even with all the people and stimulation in the streets, I felt a sense of ease in Hong Kong. It felt like home.

I was still a big-city Hong Kong boy at heart. I never really lost my Asian-ness; I just covered it up with an American façade. In Hong Kong, I didn't have to answer the question "Am I Chinese or am I American?" anymore. I was just another person. I was just me. The weight of being an immigrant and the weight of being defined as an Asian American were gone. Things that seemed like stereotypes in America were just normal in Hong Kong. Instead of an Asian guy eating weird chicken feet at the stereotypical dim sum, I was just a guy having lunch. I had forgotten that there was a place in this world where I wasn't judged for my ethnicity, and I was the norm. I felt at peace.

I visited longtime family friends at the Shanghai Club, where they served some of the most authentic Shanghainese cuisine. I visited my grand-uncle Frank, who has always been a baller wearing Italian suits. He took me to an exclusive membership-only restaurant called the American Club. I know it was ironic to fly seven thousand miles to Hong Kong just to go to the American Club, but that was the best rib-eye I've ever had on any side of the world. It was dry-aged USDA prime beef mixed with the culinary skills of the top chefs in Hong Kong.

I walked down the street I grew up on, Tin Hau Miu Road. The twenty-five-story yellowish apartment building still looked exactly the same. The giant tree on the block looked just as big as on my first day of elementary school. Maybe it grew proportionately to my size. I walked down the steps to the Tin Hau temple. I used to be so scared of the statues of Chinese mytho-logical characters in front of the temple when I was a kid; now they just looked like ugly cartoon characters. I sat down in front of the temple and was immediately bitten by a mosquito, a fa-miliar pest in the humidity of Hong Kong. The itch reminded me of my childhood summers. I went over to the Chinese phar-macy for some herbal mosquito cream. The pharmacy had ev-erything from Tylenol to Chinese herbs to a glass container filled with dried scallops, a signature Hong Kong delicacy. The place smelled like fish jerky wrapped in a Band-Aid. I strolled past the sneaker store where my dad bought me my first pair of Jordans. It was a pair of Jordan XIIs that came out in the 1996–97 NBA season when Michael Jordan defeated the Utah Jazz in the NBA finals. Those fresh J's made me easily the coolest kid in my school that year. On the same street, I found one of our favorite hole-in-the-wall restaurants that specialized in beef brisket soup. They have been perfecting the brisket for forty years, and it's the only thing they make in that restaurant. A bite of that tender brisket brought me right back to my first soccer practice in nearby Vic-toria Park, where my mom rewarded me with that brisket soup.

Everything was just as good as I remembered.

Just a few months before the trip, I reconnected with a couple of my grade school friends from Hong Kong through Facebook. My old classmate Ku Chun came across my stand-up set from *The Arsenio Hall Show* on YouTube. In the set I talked about being from Hong Kong, so he looked me up on Wikipedia and found my Chinese name. I was indeed the same kid he sat next to in third grade. So Ku friended me on Facebook, and through him I also reconnected with Darren Tse, one of my best friends from Hong Kong. I couldn't believe they managed to find me after all those years. I tried to stay in touch with them when I first moved to America, but it was the year 2000. It was before Facebook, FaceTime calls and even MySpace. I had to use my mom's international phone card to chat with my friends back in Hong Kong. I was only thirteen years old; I didn't know how to properly stay in touch with my long-distance friends. So we slowly all faded away from each other's lives. After seventeen years, we were about to hang out in Hong Kong, thanks to Arsenio Hall.

I met up with Ku and Darren at a hotel bar on top of central Hong Kong. When I walked in to find them, I had no idea who to look for. I had no idea what they looked like after all those years. I have seen puberty turn an ugly duckling into a swan, and I've also seen it turn a cute kid into a Ninja Turtle. I almost went up to two random dudes and gave them a hug. Then I heard "Jimmy!" I turned around and saw the same kids I played tag with in third grade. They were still the same guys. Ku was still the bad boy with a cool haircut; Darren was still the nice kid with a gracious smile. Chatting with them in Cantonese brought back all the memories we had in grade school. We chatted about our jobs, girlfriends we'd had and our other old friends from school. I thought I'd walk into the bar as the cool dude who made it in Hollywood, but I was pretty sure they were both making way more money than I was. Ku now runs a successful arcade business in Hong Kong, and he has a healthy collection of Ferraris and Lamborghinis; and Darren works at one of the top investment banking firms, and he just bought a multimillion-dollar condo in Hong Kong. They were the real *Crazy Rich Asians;* I was just an actor pretending to be them. But all that didn't matter; we were just happy to see each other after all these years.

When I came home to LA from Hong Kong, I felt like I had left my real home to come back to the place I called home. Before I was ever an immigrant, before I was an Asian American, I was just a kid who didn't know what either of those things meant. I've spent my entire adult life figuring out how to American. Fitting in became the only consistent part of my life. And no matter how American I tried to be, I'd always felt like an outsider. And no matter how long ago I left Hong Kong, it would always feel like home. My trip to Hong Kong gave me a chance to define myself as more than just the Asian guy in America, to see past my own ethnicity and evaluate what I'm really about. I am not the thirteen-year-old Hong Kong Jimmy anymore, and I'll never be the all-American guy; I am an amalgamation of both. I am a Chinese American Hong Kong–born immigrant who learned English from BET. If it wasn't for my family, I would not have emigrated from Hong Kong to Los Angeles, and if it wasn't for the American mindset of pursuing what I love, I would not have been a stand-up comedian. I don't have to be solely defined by where I came from, and I am more than just where I end up. I am as Chinese as I am American.

Can I see myself living in Hong Kong again? The people are great, the food is amazing and it's one of the most vibrant cities in the world. But there is one very important thing that America has to offer. The same thing that made my family and so many others before us immigrate to America: boundless opportunities. That is what makes the American dream uniquely American.

When I quit finance to become a stand-up comedian, my parents thought I was a crazy person. And they were right; I would be considered insane anywhere else in the world, except in America. Americans are encouraged to dream big and do anything we set our minds to. The United States is the only country where the pursuit of happiness is the right of its citizens. Jay-Z went from the Marcy Projects to drinking champagne on a yacht and marrying Beyoncé. I went from struggling with the English language to doing stand-up comedy and becoming a Hollywood actor. There might always be ignorant people who wish I'd go back to where I came from, but I embrace America the same way it has embraced me as its citizen. My American dream is as real as it comes.

EPILOGUE

can now find the humor when I look back at my first day of school in America, but it wasn't very funny for the thirteen-year-old Chinese boy who had to navigate through the alien world at the time. He was lost, he was scared, he wanted to go home.

It was hard.

Every immigrant has gone through a difficult journey. My story is just one out of a million stories of people who left their home country hoping for a better future. I wish I could go back in time and tell the little thirteen-year-old Jimmy that everything was going to be just fine. He probably wouldn't even believe what I'd tell him. "Jimmy, you are going to watch a lot of BET and start a rap group called Yellow Panthers. Then you'll completely disappoint your parents and become a stand-up comedian, used car salesman and strip club DJ. But don't worry, because you'll eventually come back around and get on an HBO show called *Silicon Valley!*" My thirteen-year-old self would probably stare at me blankly and ask, "What is BET? What is stand-up comedian? Who are you?"

From eating at El Pollo Loco salsa bar to the Golden Globes buffet, I managed to stumble through this journey with the perseverance of an immigrant and the mindset of an American. I learned to thrive on being uncomfortable to pursue what I loved. The English language was uncomfortable, so I studied BET until it became my natural tongue. Doing stand-up was uncomfortable, so I hung out at the Comedy Palace until it became my second home. Auditions were uncomfortable, so I spent six hundred bucks a month on acting classes while I slept in some dude's living room for three hundred bucks until acting became my profession. I never looked at these challenges as barriers; I saw them as opportunities to grow. I'd rather try to pursue my dream knowing that I might fail miserably than to have never tried at all. That is How to American.

PROUD ASIAN SON

I wrote this book in LA, NYC, Chicago, Atlanta, Paris, London, Edinburgh, Kuala Lumpur, Singapore and Hong Kong. I am grateful that comedy and acting have taken me to these places and allowed me to be here today. I have to constantly pinch myself to realize that this is not a pipe dream anymore. No matter how many different roles I play, the inside always feels the same. I'm still the same kid who grew up in Hong Kong, the same kid who didn't understand "What's up?" and the same kid who fucked up cooking the rice.

It was the most special occasion to be able to share the big screen with my dad on *Patriots Day*. I finally felt like a proud Asian son who was able to give back to my family. Sharing the same screen with my dad, Mark Wahlberg and Kevin Bacon was the epitome of the American experience. After the *Patriots Day* premiere, I finally asked my dad:

> "Dad, are you proud of me?"
> He replied earnestly, "In a Chinese family we don't have to say it all the time. You should know that I'm always proud of you." Deep down, I knew that, it was just nice to hear him say it.

My mom has since moved back to LA, where she lives with my dad in their newly purchased home. It is our family's very first house. Last year they also got our family's very first dog, the cutest pug puppy, and my parents named her Toffee, because, well, "It just sounded pretty good, like Jimmy." When we were looking to get a dog, my dad vehemently said, "I don't like dogs. You guys can go get a dog, but I won't help you take care of it." Two months later, he was making Toffee a home-cooked Shanghainese meal every day. To see the affection my mom and dad have for Toffee, I realized how good I had it when I was growing up. Even though we might never say "I love you" to each other in Chinese culture, there is so much love in these two human beings

I truly hit the lottery in life to have them as my parents. My dad once told me:

> "Having you as my son is like winning the lottery . . . Not the Mega Millions jackpot, but like a small twenty-dollar prize."

Some things never change.